# MID-ATLANTIC
## FRUIT & VEGETABLE GARDENING

*Plant, Grow, and Harvest
the Best Edibles*

First published in 2013 by Cool Springs Press, an imprint of the Quayside Publishing Group, 400 First Avenue North, Suite 400, Minneapolis, MN 55401

The information in this book is true and complete to the best of our knowledge. All recommendations are made without any guarantee on the part of the author or Publisher, who also disclaims any liability incurred in connection with the use of this data or specific details.

Cool Springs Press titles are also available at discounts in bulk quantity for industrial or sales-promotional use. For details write to Special Sales Manager at Cool Springs Press, 400 First Avenue North, Suite 400, Minneapolis, MN 55401, USA. To find out more about our books, visit us online at www.coolspringspress.com.

Library of Congress Cataloging-in-Publication Data

Elzer-Peters, Katie.
  Mid-Atlantic fruit & vegetable gardening : plant, grow, and harvest the best edibles / Katie Elzer-Peters.
     p. cm.--(Fruit & vegetable gardening)
  Other title: Mid-Atlantic fruit and vegetable gardening
  Includes index.
  ISBN 978-1-59186-564-3 (softcover)
  1. Gardening--Middle Atlantic States. 2. Fruit--Middle Atlantic States 3. Vegetable gardening--Middle Atlantic States.   I. Title. II. Title: Mid-Atlantic fruit and vegetable gardening. III. Series: Fruit & vegetable gardening

  SB451.34.M52E49 2013
  635.0974--dc23

                    2013019496

Acquisitions Editor: Mark Johanson
Design Manager: Cindy Samargia Laun
Layout: S. E. Anderson

Printed in China

10 9 8 7 6 5 4 3 2 1

# MID-ATLANTIC
## FRUIT & VEGETABLE GARDENING

*Plant, Grow, and Harvest
the Best Edibles*

## KATIE ELZER-PETERS

COOL
SPRINGS
PRESS
*Home and Garden Experts*™

MINNEAPOLIS, MINNESOTA

# CONTENTS

# PART II

# DEDICATION

*For Dr. Swasey, red pen and all.*

# ACKNOWLEDGMENTS

I always liked to write, but without the patient instruction of Mrs. Wilhoite, Mrs. Quandt, Mrs. Libby, Dr. Swasey, Dr. Garrison, and a graduate student teacher at Purdue whose name I've long forgotten, but whose influence was enormous, I would not be the same person today, and would not have the privilege to do what I do. Billie Brownell has continued to nurture my writing over the past few years, and I appreciate all of the insights and improvements she has helped me make. Billie, I hear your voice in my ear when I write—and that's a good thing.

My thanks go to Roger Waynick, original Publisher of Cool Springs Press, and to Mark Johanson, my Acquiring Editor for this project, each for taking a chance on me.

Once you start working on a book, there are people along the way that take the word doc and make it into a beautiful book. For that I have to thank the copy editors and designers and hort editors and indexers for their work. Without them, it's all just words on the computer that might or might not make sense, and are certainly not very interesting to look at.

Every writer needs a cheerleader, and Tracy Stanley at Cool Springs has been that and more. She is the most patient, encouraging, and helpful editor one could ask for. This has been much easier with you to help me. Thank you so much, Tracy!

The Owner and Chef of Epic Food Co., James Bain, along with his staff, have been so friendly and nice, allowing me to camp out, drink their tea, eat their chocolate chip cookies, steal their WiFi, and devour their glorious vegetable creations while working on this book. Thank you.

And I couldn't do anything without the love and support of my parents, who never said no when I wanted them to buy me a book and my husband—chief garden-waterer and dog wrangler in the house. Joe, you have the patience of a saint, and I'm glad you're mine.

# PREFACE

I have been gardening since I could walk, and I have enjoyed, throughout my professional career, teaching others how to garden.

When faced with the task of making vegetable gardening an easily digestible (pun intended) topic for new gardeners, I tried to come up with a method of organization that differed from the usual A–Z list of plants.

## *Organization by Function, Not Name*

Gardens don't grow well when alphabetized. I know this because I've tried to plant alphabet vegetable gardens for kids. The cucumbers end up growing all over the beets, and the grapes shade the eggplants. It's messy. So why should your gardening book be organized that way? Sure, it's easy to look things up alphabetically, but what if the book, through the way it is organized, could help you plan your garden?

Now we're talking! (There's always the index and the alpha-order plant list to help you look up the location of your favorite veggie's information.)

In the Mid-Atlantic, you can garden year-round. Greens and root crops flourish in the winter, and tropical vegetables such as tomatoes and peppers thrive during the hot summer. This book has sections covering cool-season gardening and warm-season gardening.

Your fruit or vegetable garden doesn't need to be this big in order for you to enjoy fresh produce!

A few holes in the leaves of this eggplant plant won't affect the fruit.

It isn't just weather you have to be concerned about, though. The plant families (stone fruits, cabbage relatives) and their growth habits (tree, shrub, vine) also influence where you plant them and how you grow them. The fruits section is organized by growth habit to make it easy for you to figure out where to plant the plants so that they produce well for you without taking over your entire garden.

Hopefully this admittedly unusual style will help when you're ready to put shovel to soil. Just open to the section you want to tackle and go!

## Never Too Ugly to Eat

If there's one piece of advice I could give to any new gardener—the one thing you can't ignore—it is this: your garden doesn't have to be gorgeous to produce well. Your tomato plant could look like it is on its last legs, but if it is still flowering and pumping out tomatoes, don't sweat it.

The eggplant leaves might have spots. The eggplants will probably be fine. Just because you see a few holes here and there doesn't mean you need to bring out the big guns and spray everything.

If you see aphids on the plants, get out the hose and spray them. If that doesn't work, try insecticidal soap. (Read on to learn how to deal with aphids and other pests.) If you see a giant tomato hornworm, pluck it and squash it. But don't feel discouraged if your garden doesn't look like a magazine cover. Is what you're growing tasty? Good. That's what you're going for.

Now get out there and get your hands dirty! Get the book dirty, too! That's what it's for.

—Katie

# GROWING EDIBLES IN THE MID-ATLANTIC

I firmly believe that if you understand how plants grow, you'll take better care of them and have better results. It isn't enough to know just the how-to. To be successful at

gardening, you also need to know the why-do. With a bit of information, gardening suddenly goes from mysterious to predictable. You'll learn that if you prune a plant *this way* it will grow *that way*.

Part I of this book gives you everything you need to know to grow the best edibles in your home garden.

Carrots are easy to grow in the Mid-Atlantic.

Scarlet runner beans growing up trellises are as pretty as they are tasty!

You'll learn about:

**Gardening within the Mid-Atlantic**—regional differences in soil, rainfall, temperature, and so on

**Seasonal gardening**—what it means and how to make the most of each season

**Garden planning**—getting the most out of your space, large or small

**Soil**—the most important part of every garden, and the trickiest aspects of gardening in the Mid-Atlantic

**Selecting plants**—varieties for our area, whether to buy transplants or seeds, and how to plant them

**Growing and maintaining the garden**—how to water, when to fertilize, what to use for mulch, how to deal with pests, and so forth

# USDA PLANT HARDINESS ZONE MAPS

## *Delaware, District of Columbia, Maryland Pennsylvania, Virginia, and West Virginia*

The USDA Plant Hardiness Zone Map indicates the average minimum cold temperatures for regions. The map was reissued in 2012 and reflects a warming trend affecting gardeners.

All plant labels and catalogs list hardiness zones to aid in plant selection—particularly trees, shrubs, and perennial herbs and vegetables. A plant is considered "hardy" in a zone if it can withstand the average minimum temperature in that area. If your area is too cold for a plant to live through winter, you can still grow it as an annual. Hardiness zones are not as applicable to annual vegetables, such as tomatoes or peppers, that you grow for only one season.

Sow pea seeds for a fall cover crop.

There are other temperature-related factors affecting plant growth other than annual minimum temperature, including:

**Chilling hours:** hours below 45°F, mostly related to fruit production

**Heat:** extreme summer heat that causes blossom drop in vegetables

**Temperature fluctuation:** which can cause bolting and flowering in cool-season crops

These factors are explained later in the book. Because all plant labels indicate plant hardiness, they are a good place to start in learning how to pick out the right plants.

Look at the hardiness zone map and see which zone corresponds to your area. Remember both the zone number and the temperature range—they will come in handy when selecting plants.

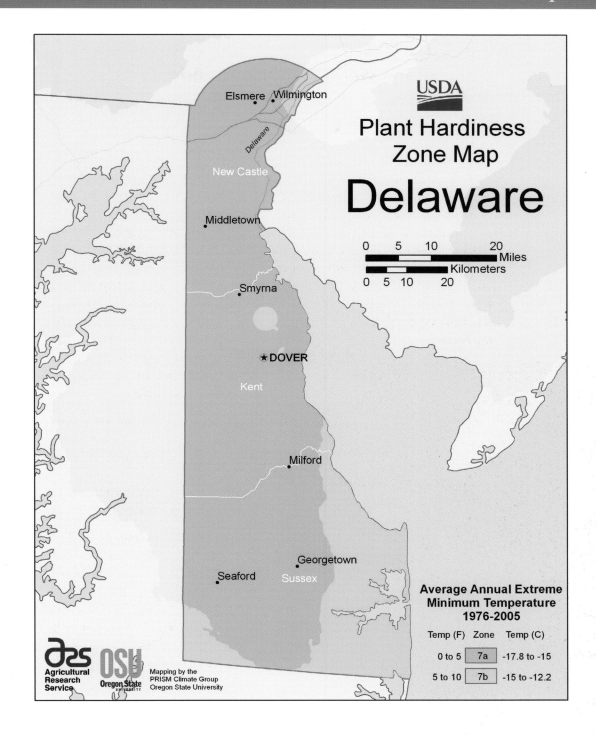

USDA Plant Hardiness Zone Map, 2012. Agricultural Research Service, U.S. Department of Agriculture. Accessed from http://planthardiness.ars.usda.gov.

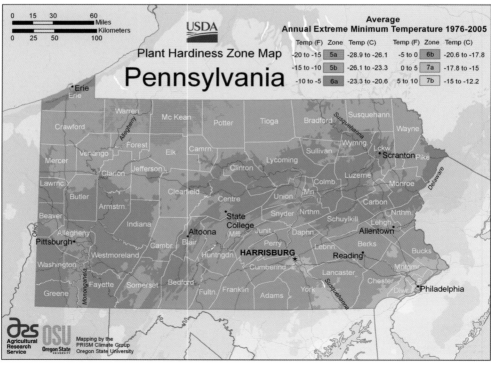

USDA Plant Hardiness Zone Map, 2012. Agricultural Research Service, U.S. Department of Agriculture. Accessed from http://planthardiness.ars.usda.gov.

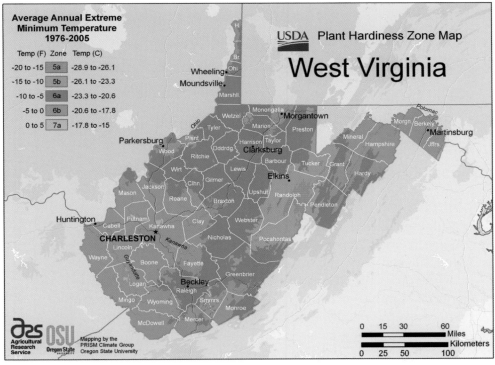

USDA Plant Hardiness Zone Map, 2012. Agricultural Research Service, U.S. Department of Agriculture. Accessed from http://planthardiness.ars.usda.gov.

# CHAPTER 1

# THE MID-ATLANTIC REGION

Gardeners in the Mid-Atlantic experience hot, humid summers and cool to cold winters within USDA hardiness zones 5b through 8a. Northern Pennsylvania and mountainous areas of Virginia and West Virginia are the coldest. The coastal plain sections of Virginia, Delaware, and Maryland along the Chesapeake Bay and Atlantic Ocean are the warmest. Cold weather isn't the only factor influencing gardening, though. Soil types, humidity, summer heat, and geographical features also influence plant growth.

These gardening conditions, from soil to weather, are directly related to where you live.

## Soils in the Mid-Atlantic

In addition to cold weather, the other big variation in the Mid-Atlantic is in soil types. Soil is composed of three types of particles: sand, silt, and clay. Sand is the coarsest particle in soil and clay is the finest particle. The mixture of these three types of particles is what gives soil its structure and texture. That, in turn, affects the water-holding and nutrient-holding capacity of the soil and its suitability as-is for growing plants.

Soil types have a big impact on plant growth, but, unfortunately, it's almost impossible to generalize about soil types because soil characteristics vary widely. In the Mid-Atlantic you can have sandy soil (near the coast) to mucky soil in lowlands, to heavy clay in some areas of the mountains and Allegheny Plateau. Because soil characteristics have a major impact on plant growth and health, it is worth learning about the specific type of soil you're working with in your garden.

## Gardening Regions in the Mid-Atlantic

These regions are primarily divided based on hardiness zones, proximity to the ocean or mountains, and soil types. There is however, a huge variation in growing conditions in each region. For specific growing information related to your city, consult with your local garden club or cooperative extension office.

## Coastal Plain

Areas of the Mid-Atlantic referred to as "The Coastal Plain" include the entire state of Delaware, as well as areas of Pennsylvania, Maryland, and Virginia that are within 100 miles of the Chesapeake Bay or Atlantic Ocean. These are some of the warmest areas covered by this book. Coastal plain areas have sandier soils, generally, than other areas of the Mid-Atlantic, but there are pockets of clay and muck soils. The Coastal Plain region also experiences the most distinct separation of cool-season and warm-season gardening. Summers are hot and humid. Winters are cool, but not frigid. This area can get snow during the winter.

**Hardiness zones:** 6a–8a

**Soil characteristics:** Range from extremely fast-draining near the water to mucky lowland soils to heavy clay in higher elevation areas.

**Unique issues:** Ice storms in the winter, which can damage trees and shrubs. Salt spray from the bay or ocean can damage plant leaves and soil. Periods of warm weather during the winter can impact dormancy of fruit trees.

## Mountains

Mountains are found in every Mid-Atlantic state except for Delaware. Coldest areas of the mountains include high elevations in West Virginia and central Pennsylvania between State College and Pittsburgh. These are some of the coldest areas of the Mid-Atlantic. Cool- and warm-season gardening is more compressed in these areas.

**Hardiness zones:** 5a–6b

**Soil characteristics:** Soils in the mountains of the Mid-Atlantic region are mostly well-drained sandy or silty loam. There are often rock fragments in the soil. In some areas, the topsoil isn't very deep. Gardeners with shallow soils might consider growing vegetables in raised beds.

**Unique issues:** Many of the mountainous areas are shaded. Availability of full-day sunlight can be a challenge in some gardens. The growing season in the highest elevations and coldest areas is also shorter than any other area. It is important for gardeners in the mountains to carefully read plant labels and to grow varieties well-suited to their number of frost-free days.

## Interior Foothills-Piedmont

The Interior Foothills and Piedmont region includes most of Virginia (between the mountains and Coastal Plain), Pennsylvania between Lancaster and Philadelphia, and Maryland between Baltimore and Hagerstown. This region is characterized by rolling hills and valleys with differing soil conditions depending upon the topography. Summers are humid and winters are cool.

**Hardiness zones:** 6b–8a

**Soil characteristics:** Soils in this area range from loamy, limestone-based soils in the valleys to acidic shale or sandstone-based soils on the hilltops. Soil quality varies highly within the region.

**Unique issues:** Hot, humid summers can be beneficial for fungal and bacterial diseases (and thus a problem for the gardener). Winters are cool—colder in the northern areas (Pennsylvania) of this region than in southern areas (Virginia).

## Allegheny and Pittsburgh Plateau

The Allegheny and Pittsburgh Plateau stretches from southern West Virginia, through Western Pennsylvania, and across the top of Pennsylvania. Cold winters, humid summers, and a shorter season characterize this region.

**Hardiness zones:** 5a–6b

**Soil characteristics:** Sandy loam and silty loam soils are common in this area.

**Unique issues:** These areas can experience heavy winter and lake-effect snows.

## How to Use Frost Tables

Seed packets and plant labels usually have language that refers to the average last-frost date or the average first-frost date, such as:

- Plant inside six to eight weeks before the average last frost. Transplant outside after danger of frost has passed.
- Sow seeds directly outside twelve weeks before the last frost.

Frost tables refer more to the length of different portions of the gardening season than to the severity of the winter, as the USDA hardiness zones do. Use frost tables to judge when to plant cool-season crops to take advantage of cool weather and to plan for warm-season crops during the time of the year they grow best. Frost tables are organized by city.

Because of the variation in frost-free dates from region to region, it's best to just look up frost data for your city here.

## Frost Tables by City

| City | Last Probable Spring Freeze | First Probable Fall Freeze | Probable Number of Frost-Free Days |
|---|---|---|---|
| Washington, DC | Apr. 20 | Nov. 2 | 207 |
| Dover, DE | May 1 | Oct. 18 | 181 |
| Lewes, DE | Apr. 20 | Oct. 30 | 205 |
| Milford, DE | May 8 | Oct. 16 | 181 |
| Newark, DE | May 14 | Oct. 12 | 164 |
| Wilmington, DE | May 7 | Oct. 16 | 175 |
| Annapolis, MD | May 3 | Oct. 23 | 186 |
| Baltimore, MD | May 8 | Oct. 17 | 175 |
| Salisbury, MD | May 6 | Oct. 21 | 182 |
| Allentown, PA | May 14 | Oct. 8 | 158 |
| Erie, PA | May 30 | Oct. 15 | 154 |
| Lancaster, PA | May 17 | Oct 6 | 162 |
| Philadelphia, PA | Apr. 27 | Oct. 26 | 193 |
| Pittsburgh, PA | May 30 | Oct. 5 | 145 |
| Uniontown, PA | June 6 | Sept. 25 | 128 |
| Colonial Beach, VA | Apr. 28 | Nov. 6 | 188 |
| Lynchburg, VA | May 12 | Oct. 11 | 165 |
| Norfolk, VA | Apr. 6 | Nov. 27 | 217 |
| Reston, VA | May 21 | Oct. 5 | 150 |
| Richmond, VA | May 7 | Oct. 20 | 181 |
| Roanoke, VA | May 14 | Oct. 8 | 161 |
| Charleston, WV | May 19 | Oct. 11 | 160 |
| Martinsburg, WV | May 18 | Oct. 6 | 155 |
| Parkersburg, WV | May 21 | Oct. 9 | 158 |

# CHAPTER 2

# SEASONAL GARDENING

Most edible plants that we grow fall into two categories: cool season plants (that grow best when temperatures are cool—usually below 70°F) and warm season plants (that grow best when temperatures are warmer—usually above 65°F). In the Mid-Atlantic, the Coastal Plain and Foothills regions have a longer growing season with more distinct cool and warm growing seasons than either the Mountains or Allegheny Plateau. Cooler areas have a more compressed growing season.

While many gardening books for this region do not divide plants (or gardening seasons) into warm and cool, for newer gardeners, that distinction is helpful. Success in gardening starts with planting, and putting plants in the ground at the right time, or starting seeds inside at the right time for transplanting outside is vital. Even if the time between planting a cool-season plant such as broccoli, and a warm-season plant such as a tomato is only a month or two, those two months can make a big difference.

For the most part, "cool" and "warm" are apt descriptors for the conditions that certain plants like. The two seasons have another defining factor beyond temperature, though, and that is light. There is less daylight and a longer night during the cool season. There is more daylight and a shorter night during the warm season.

It just so happens that one of the cool-season plants everyone enjoys eating, spinach, is also a long-day plant that flowers when the days are long and the nights are short. That's good for gardeners because we don't want spinach to flower when we're

### BIENNIAL VEGETABLES

Some plants defy neat categorizing—they grow equally well in warm weather and cold weather. These plants are considered to be biennial. They won't flower and set seed until their second year. Swiss chard and arugula are the two main traditional "cool weather" vegetables that will grow just fine throughout summer if they are planted in spring. Kale will  grow throughout summer, as well, though the leaves can be tough and bitter during hotter weather.

Swiss chard is a biennial vegetable.

growing it to eat. We just want lots of tender leaves. It's funny how that works!

For the most part, you don't have to worry about day length in the vegetable garden—temperature serves as an easier-to-manage limiting factor. However, if you find yourself having difficulty with a plant and you're sure that you've gotten everything else right, look up more information (university extension websites are good places to check) to see if day length is a factor in the way it grows. You might be beating your head against the wall for no reason.

Cold and heat *both* influence plants. This concept can be confusing to gardeners, because most plant labeling covers only USDA hardiness zones, and those zones relate to cold and not heat. Zones are useful for only one temperature-related bit of information: whether the plant can withstand the coldest air temperatures likely to occur in a region.

There are many other temperature-related factors—beyond cold hardiness—that affect plant growth, including soil temperature, air temperatures (beyond the minimum temperature), and fluctuation in temperatures. Temperature affects when you can plant, when plants will flower and fruit, and when you need to harvest fruits and vegetables.

## Cool-Season and Warm-Season Gardening

In the Mid-Atlantic region cool season plants thrive from March through May and again in September through November. (Dates vary depending on where you live.) The warm season runs from May (in the warmest areas) or June through September. If you plan your Mid-Atlantic garden around no other guiding principle than this, you will be well in front of people who don't. The simple fact is:

- Cool-season herbs and vegetables do not grow well throughout the summer. You'll frustrate yourself endlessly if you try to make them do so. The same goes for trying to grow warm-season vegetables and herbs in cooler weather.
- Just because the stores stock tomato transplants in March doesn't mean you should plant them outside in March.

Most of the edible plants we grow came from somewhere else besides North America. Blueberries are native, as are cranberries. Their history provides clues to the conditions in which they grow best:

- Cabbage, and cabbage-family plants (brassicas) were domesticated as garden plants in cooler, northern regions of Europe. Cabbages enjoy long, cool, but not cold, winters in the Mid-Atlantic.
- Tomatoes are native to tropical highlands and are long, perennial vines in their natural habitat. We grow them as summer annuals during the warm season of our more temperate climate. Once a frost hits, they're done.

## Bolting

When cool-season vegetables, most of which are true "vegetables" (we eat the vegetative parts of the plants—leaves, roots, stems), move from the vegetative stage of growth to the flowering stage of growth—an action called bolting— it's time to stop eating them. All of a sudden, from the nice little clump of lettuce leaves you've been picking, a long stem starts to grow. Then flowers appear. The plant has bolted, and it is completing its life cycle, ending in flowering and seed production.

Collard plants bolting (flowering and producing seeds).

Lettuces, cabbages, broccoli, cauliflower, turnips, and radishes are all vegetables that will bolt. Dill and cilantro are two cool-season herbs that bolt. (Unlike lettuce seeds, though, dill seeds and cilantro seeds (coriander) are useful in the kitchen.) Most cool season crops will bolt in the spring, as the days get longer and the temperatures get warmer.

Broccoli plants bolting. The part of the broccoli that we eat is the flower. Once the broccoli heads start to grow and bloom, the window of harvest is over.

### Spring Bolting

Any cool-weather plants that you planted in fall or early spring have the potential to bolt in late spring as the temperatures warm up and the days get longer. Resist the urge to keep your fall-planted cabbages in the garden for too long in spring, because they will start to crack and flower. Pick broccoli heads when they are still tight. The part of broccoli that we eat is actually the plant's undeveloped flower head. If you let the heads sit in the garden, they will start to stretch out and bloom.

## Soil Temperature

You can buy an inexpensive soil thermometer to help you gauge when to plant different edibles. Cool-season vegetables germinate well when the soil is at least 50°F. Most will sprout when soil temperatures are 50°F to 70°F. Warm-season vegetables grow best when soil temperatures are at least 65°F. You can plant these when soil temperatures are lower, but the plants won't grow.

Diseases are also more of a problem in cool, wet soils. Sweet corn seeds will rot in the ground if planted too early, while the soil is still cold. Damping off, pythium, and root rot diseases can strike seeds that are planted too early in the year, when the soil hasn't warmed up yet.

Soil thermometer

## Biological Indicators

If you read older gardening books, you'll sometimes see directions with biological indicators rather than dates. There might be instructions to plant a certain vegetable" when the redbuds are in bloom." Rather than using dates as an indicator of when to plant, these instructions use what's going on in the world around the garden as information for timing of planting. You can learn your own indicators. Observe what's happening in and around the vegetable garden when you plant certain plants. Over the years, you'll learn that you will sow your last crop of lettuce when the azaleas are blooming, and you'll harvest your first strawberries when the daylilies start flowering.

### Tropical Annual Edibles Like It Hot

These favorite summer vegetables are native to tropical areas and grow only when soil temperatures are warm enough (at least 65°F). Don't plant these too early:

| | | |
|---|---|---|
| Bean | Pepper | Sweet potato |
| Corn | Potato | Tomatillo |
| Cucumber | Pumpkin | Tomato |
| Eggplant | Summer squash | Watermelon |

## Air Temperature

Cold air can be shocking to new transplants. Extremely hot air (85°F and hotter) will cause flowers to drop off tomatoes, reducing the eventual tomato harvest. Some plants (many fruit trees) need a certain number of hours below 45°F in order to produce fruit. Beyond a killing freeze, here's what you need to know about air temperature and plant growth.

### Chilling Hours

Some plants not only like, they *need* colder air. Most fruit trees need a certain number of hours with air temperatures below 45°F, called chilling hours. Plants with chilling hour requirements must meet the minimum number of chilling hours in order to break dormancy and bloom. (Remember: no blooms, no fruits!) During warmer winters, fruit trees can get physiologically "confused," blooming early, late, or not at all.

Corn plants roll up their leaves to prevent water loss.

**WHAT'S WRONG WITH MY CORN?**

When corn plants don't have enough water available to take up (the soil is too dry), they will roll their leaves up to reduce the amount of surface area exposed, thus lowering the amount of water lost through the leaves. If the corn leaves are rolled up and "pointy," you need to water the plants!

### Heat and Fruit Set

Heat, the other side of the thermometer, affects fruit set in a favorite garden crop: tomatoes. When daytime temperatures rise above 85°F, tomato flowers fall off the plants without being pollinated. No flowers means no fruit.

## Temperature Variations within the Mid-Atlantic

Elevation, latitude, and proximity to the coast (and the moderating effects of the ocean) all contribute to temperature differences between areas within the Mid-Atlantic. There can be as many as two months between the optimum tomato-planting time in Harrisburg, Pennsylvania, and that in Richmond, Virginia. Do your homework before deciding what to plant and when.

# CHAPTER 3

# PLANNING YOUR GARDEN

Plan before you plant. It's easier to imagine everything on paper than it is to relocate it once you've put shovel to soil.

## Where to Put Vegetable Beds

Sunlight is the biggest limiting factor in where you can put your vegetable beds. Keep in mind that where the sun is during winter and during summer are two different things. For one thing, sun hits places in winter that it doesn't reach in summer, because deciduous trees have lost their leaves. The sun is also at a higher angle in the sky in summer than in winter, which means that shadows created by things such as houses or fences fall in different places.

Planting edible trees or shrubs along a lot line is a good way to use this space and a friendlier way to mark the edge of your property than a fence.

There are also other factors to consider when placing the vegetable garden:

**Your sightline and the traffic patterns around your house:** If your vegetable beds are stuck in a back corner where you don't have to view them or walk by them regularly, you'll pay a lot less attention to them, which is not good for your plants.

**Proximity to a hose hookup:** It is (literally) a drag to have to run 100 feet of hose across sidewalks and through a garden gate to get to the vegetable garden. (Trust me, I've done it. I do it. I have no other choice because of where the sun hits my yard.)

**Location of garden tools:** The closer you can get the bed to the tools, the easier it will be to do maintenance.

Take it from someone who has had to break all three of these rules to get a vegetable garden in her yard: if you can, follow the above tips.

### To Fence or Not to Fence?

Whether or not you should fence your vegetable garden is a matter of preference and necessity. If you have deer problems, absolutely look into some kind of fencing—but it had better be tall! If you don't have critter problems (two-legged or four-legged), a fence can be more of a pain than a help. For one thing, it can block sunlight. Fencing can also be expensive. I side with the "not to fence" crowd, unless you can't grow vegetables without one.

### Electric Fence for Vegetable Gardens

If you have bad pressure from deer in the area, you can put up an electric fence that's relatively unobtrusive. Fiberglass rods and a single electrified strand will do it. The trick is, you have to bait the fence by clipping foil-wrapped peanut butter to the electrified wire. The only way to train the deer to stay away from a single-strand fence is to make them put their tongue on it. All it takes is one time—then they'll stay away.

## Siting Fruit Trees and Shrubs

I like to plant my fruit trees and bramble shrubs along the edges of my property. Primarily, that's because it's the only place I have room. If you're planning to plant fruit trees and shrubs in an older subdivision, you might find that the only areas you have to work with, without having to uproot a bunch of other plants, are the edges of your property. That's fine! It's nicer (and less expensive) to put up a "fence" of blackberries than an actual fence. Once fruit trees start to bear, they can also be messy. (It's impossible to get all of the fruit from the tree into the harvest basket—there will be some that ends up on the ground.) Keeping the trees in one, concentrated area makes cleanup of the rest of your yard easier.

Sage varieties line a short pathway outside the kitchen door. By planting herbs close to the kitchen, you'll be sure to use them more.

## Incorporating Edibles into the Landscape

Some edibles are easier to plant in the landscape than others. If you aren't ripping out your entire front yard to turn it into a vegetable garden, but you have limited space, you can plant certain edibles as foundation plantings or in the flower beds. Overall it is a lot easier to care for vegetables and fruits if they're in one location, but if you have the opportunity to redo your landscaping, or you want to shoehorn in some extra plants, these are some edibles that play well with others:

**Blueberries:** In addition to their tasty fruits, these deciduous shrubs have beautiful red fall color.

**Apples and cherries:** These early-spring bloomers are beautiful landscape specimens.

**Swiss chard, kale, and cabbage:** These cool-season greens are as beautiful as they are tasty. As an added bonus, chard and kale will grow in partial sun—a rarity for most edibles.

**Sorrel, fennel, dill, and parsley:** All four of these herbs will grow in full sun to partial shade, and they look quite at home in a perennial border.

**Culinary sage:** Instead of growing Mexican sage, plant culinary sage instead. You'll get the same gray-green leaf effect, but the culinary sage is edible.

**Creeping thyme:** Anywhere you need a ground cover in full sun, you can plant creeping thyme. If you happen to step on it, you'll release some of the fragrance of the leaves.

### Placing Perennial Edibles

You might decide that you want to grow some perennial edibles in your vegetable garden. You can put these vegetables and fruits wherever you

---

**GROWING TIPS**

Don't forget the pollinator trees. Not all fruit trees need a pollinator tree, but many do. For each fruit type, select a second variety of the same species that blooms around the same time as your other choices, and plant it in the same row as the others. Make sure that the pollinator tree does, in fact, produce pollen, and isn't sterile!

want, but it is a good idea to put them somewhere a bit out of the way, where you won't mind them staying put. They're all different, so there's not a "one plant fits all" solution.

Asparagus beds take up a lot of room, and the plants grow to be quite tall during summer. Globe artichokes are large plants that also get to be tall, so you could site these on the north side of the vegetable garden.

Sorrel is a shorter, decorative herb. It would be quite at home in the perennial garden or as a vegetable bed border plant.

### Perennial Edibles

| | |
|---|---|
| Asparagus | Rhubarb |
| Globe artichoke | Sorrel |
| Radicchio | Strawberry |

### The Edible Container Garden

There are entire books about edible container gardening filled with much more than we can cover in a short paragraph. If your space is limited though, or you want to grow plants that spread (mint), require switching out the soil seasonally (broccoli, cabbage), or are marginally hardy (citrus), containers are the way to go.

A lettuce bowl is a fun way to grow salad greens if you're limited on time and space.

**Lettuce bowls:** If you can't bring yourself to do a full-scale seasonal switch of your vegetable garden, planting a lettuce bowl or two is a good alternative. In two 12- or 16-inch-diameter bowls, you can grow enough lettuce to pick four to six salads a week.

**Marauding mint:** Mint will take over an entire yard in one season if allowed. Want to have fresh garnishes for your cocktails? Plant just one pot of mint—you'll have plenty.

**Broccoli and cole crops:** Plants in the cabbage family have to be rotated to different areas of the garden each year for three years. If you have raised beds, this can be difficult. Instead of planting these plants in the ground, fill a few whisky barrels with new soil each year, and plant your broccoli in there to avoid soilborne diseases.

Keep mint from taking over the garden by growing it in a pot.

## Raised-Bed Gardening

If you're interested in growing vegetables, you've probably heard about raised-bed gardening. So what's the fuss all about? Raised-bed gardening makes growing vegetables much easier for people with limited space or time, mobility challenges, or polluted soils. By gardening in raised beds, you can grow more food in less space and more easily control the soil and growing conditions, while contending with fewer weed problems.

### Assembling a Raised-Bed Kit

**1** Raised-bed kits are easy to assemble.

**2** You can fill the beds with soil or compost—no weed cloth needed.

**3** Raised beds are easy to reach and plant.

**4** You can go from zero to garden in just an hour!

## Benefits of Raised-Bed Gardening

Easy to assemble

Elevated gardening area—easier
  to reach

Less soil compaction

Soil warms up faster

Can control the quality of the soil

Can grow more in less space

Fewer weed and pest problems

## Challenges of Raised-Bed Gardening

High startup costs

Limited space for growing

Difficult to move or disassemble

## Build Your Own or Buy a Kit?

You can make your own raised-bed garden out of stacked concrete blocks, wood timbers, discarded bricks, or landscape timbers. Just about the only material you should not use to make a raised-bed garden is railroad ties. Those are treated with so many chemicals that you'd be working against yourself from the get-go.

Myth or fact? You shouldn't use treated wood to build raised-bed gardens.

Myth. The effects of treated wood extend only a few millimeters from the surface of the wood itself. Using untreated wood is a sure way to make sure you have to rebuild within a few years. If you have access to cedar planks and can afford them, you can have the best of both worlds—a wood garden bed frame with natural antirotting properties.

## Raised-Bed Maintenance

There are two types of maintenance involved in raised-bed gardening: maintaining the bed structure and maintaining the bed soil. It's a good idea to walk around the raised beds at the beginning of each year to make sure that everything is in its place. Do any nails need to be pounded in? Is there dry rot in one of the boards? Are any pieces of plastic cracked?

Because raised beds are gardened more intensely than landscape beds or row gardens, producing more food per square foot, you also need to maintain the soil. When you change over a raised bed from cool-season to warm-season vegetables and back again, add some compost to each of the beds and incorporate it into the beds with a garden claw. You can buy bagged compost or make your own. Worm castings are also a good soil additive for the beds.

## Garden Planning for Raised Beds

If your entire vegetable garden is made of raised beds, it's tempting to keep them all planted so that everything looks nice and neat. Resist the urge! The beauty of raised-bed gardens is that it is easy to move from season to season, and crop to crop, without having to get out a big rototiller to turn over a half-acre garden. Give yourself flexibility by leaving areas open. If you have six raised beds, plant two in peas in early spring. Leave two for successive plantings of lettuce and cool-season herbs. Plant one with cabbage in fall to harvest in spring, and leave one fallow so that it is ready for the first plantings of beans or tomatoes while the rest of the cool-season crops are still finishing up.

# CHAPTER 4

# BUILDING GREAT SOIL

Have you heard the phrase, "plant a five-dollar plant in a twenty-five-dollar hole"? It's true. The soil is where plants take up oxygen for the processes they need in order to grow. The soil holds and releases nutrients for the plants. Plants draw water from the soil. Characteristics of the soil make it easy or difficult for plant roots to grow, spread, and reach more water, nutrients, and oxygen. Another phrase you see often in gardening literature is, "feed the soil, not the plants." Time spent getting the soil where it needs to be in order to support healthy plant growth is time saved trying to fix problems later.

A compost bin can keep roots out of your compost and help contain the pile.

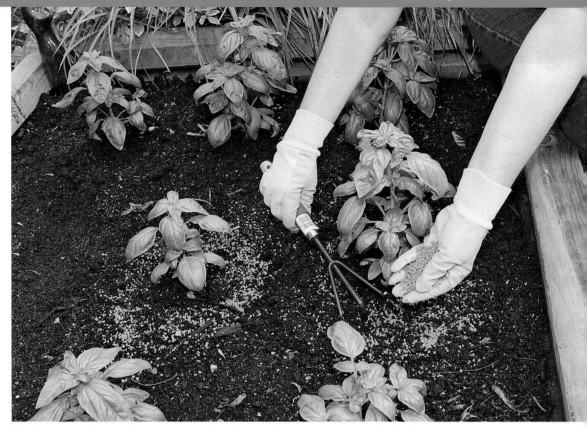

Fertilizer, whether synthetic or organic, is almost always necessary in the Mid-Atlantic.

## What You're Starting with: Soils in the Mid-Atlantic

Soils in the Mid-Atlantic vary widely. In some areas, you'll stick a shovel in the ground and find nothing but coarse sand. Other areas are plagued with sticky, slow-to-drain clay that dries to be hard as a rock during a drought. Many areas of the Mid-Atlantic are blessed with loose, well-drained, nutrient-rich loamy soils.

The pH of the soil can range from acidic (low) to alkaline (high). The only way to know what you're dealing with is to get a soil test. You can spend years building up your soil—getting the texture right, adding organic matter, and correcting the pH. What I've learned by gardening in the same place for several years is that whatever you try to do to your soil, it will try to revert back to its natural state. It's a never-ending battle.

## Add Organic Matter

Some people would tell you to test the soil before you do anything else. You can do that, but once you add compost or additional organic matter such as worm castings or blood meal, you will have changed the composition—and possibly the pH—of the soil, which makes your soil test useless.

Why would you add more compost to the soil before testing it? You can *always* add compost. Compost is the duct tape of the garden. It fixes everything!

### How to Compost

You can buy compost if you're short on time. You can (and should) also make your own. Composting is a great way to cut down on the amount of

trash you throw away. It's also a shame to have to buy something you can make yourself from food scraps, leaves, and yard debris that you otherwise have to pay someone else to take away!

### Compost Ingredients

There are two types of materials to add to compost piles: green materials, which are high in nitrogen, and brown materials, which are high in carbon. While there isn't a precise ratio of green to brown materials required in compost piles, if you add equal amounts of each over time, you'll get usable compost faster.

It's important to continually add compost to your raised beds and vegetable gardens.

Kitchen scraps

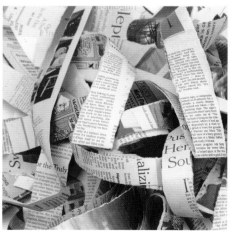

Shredded newspaper

**Green Materials**

| | |
|---|---|
| Grass clippings | Kitchen scraps |
| Weeds | Eggshells |
| Green leaves | |

**Brown Materials**

| | |
|---|---|
| Shredded newspapers | Paper towels |
| Dried leaves | Twigs |
| Sawdust | Tea bags |
| Wood chips | Wheat straw |
| Paper bags | Coffee grounds |

Grass clippings

You can compost almost any natural material, but if you're composting at home, don't put any animal products other than eggshells in the compost pile. No meat, cheese, dairy, or lasagna leftovers.

### Building the Pile

Build a compost pile by layering green materials and brown materials like you'd make a lasagna. Start with chopped-up dried leaves (you can run over them with the lawn mower). Then add grass clippings or kitchen scraps, and keep layering. The smaller the pieces you add to the pile, the faster they will decompose.

Continuously add material to the compost pile—shredded newspapers, the stems of broccoli, last summer's dead annual flowers that you pulled up, even the Halloween pumpkin.

Keep the pile "cooking" (a healthy pile will heat up) by using a pitchfork or garden fork to turn the pile, mix it up, and oxygenate it.

## Other Soil Amendments

Adding compost to the garden is always a good idea. There are other types of organic matter that you can add to the soil to provide extra nutrients to plants, either when you're planting or when you're prepping the soil for planting.

Compost pile

## Compost Troubleshooting

### Smelly Piles

Smelly compost piles are usually too wet. You can fix this by adding more brown materials and turning the pile so that it can dry out. Throw some dry, chopped leaves, straw, or shredded paper on the pile.

### Piles That Aren't Shrinking

As the items in the pile decompose, the pile will shrink. If the pile isn't shrinking, it isn't cooking. First turn the pile, and then water it. If that doesn't help—if the pile is damp but still not shrinking—add green materials to kick-start the organisms that break down the pile.

### Blood Meal and Plant-Tone

Plant-tone

Blood meal, bonemeal, and plant tones are organic, slow-release fertilizers made from animal products. Sprinkle them around the plants (this is called sidedressing) and work them into the soil with a four-tine claw. Just like synthetic fertilizers, plant tones are available for acid-loving plants, vegetables, flowers, and trees. Each type has different combinations of nutrients and ingredients to best benefit the receiving plants. Use these when you're planting to add nutrients that will break down slowly over time. Do not use them with nitrogen-fixing plants in the pea family, because you'll encourage more leaves and fewer flowers, which results in fewer peas.

### Worm Castings and Soil Conditioner

Worm castings

Worm castings (worm poop) are expensive to buy, but they're wonderful for garden plants, particularly vegetables. Worm castings and soil conditioner are similar products, in that they are both almost entirely composed of humic acid, which is the most decomposed element in soil. Humic acid is excellent for plants. Incorporate worm castings or soil conditioner into your soil before planting and you'll be amazed at how well your plants grow. You can make your own worm castings by becoming a worm farmer. Buy a worm bin, and follow the directions for procuring and feeding the worms. Worm composting is also a great way to get rid of kitchen scraps.

### Garden Soil and Topsoil

Garden soil and topsoil are coarser soils that you can use to build up areas of the garden where soil has washed away. Some bagged garden soil has slow-release fertilizer mixed into it. It's helpful to mix garden soil or topsoil with compost before planting a garden bed. The compost adds nutrients and natural water-holding components, while the topsoil adds structure and bulk. Do not buy garden soil with synthetic fertilizer in it.

Garden soil

### Manure

You can make your own compost, but you can also buy composted manure or pick it up from a horse farm. Cow, rabbit, chicken, and mushroom compost are the most commonly available types for purchase. If you get manure from a local farm, make sure that it has been sitting and aging for at least six months. Ammonia in fresh manure can burn your plants. Never use cat or dog droppings in the garden.

## Test the Soil

After you've added compost, manure, or topsoil to create the garden bed in which you'll grow your plants, it's time to test the soil. Testing now gives you a more accurate picture of the conditions the plants will have to deal with while they're growing and any additional adjustments you need to make.

Cow manure

You can get soil test boxes and forms from your county extension service. You can also purchase soil test kits at garden centers and home-improvement stores so that you can test the soil at home. These kits allow you to test for the soil's pH and the presence of nitrogen (N), phosphorus (P), and potassium (K). Test the soil to see if anything is lacking before adding fertilizer, lime, or amendments other than compost to the garden.

---

### GROWING TIP

You can pick up soil test boxes from your local Cooperative Extension office. Every test result will give you recommendations for adding nitrogen, phosphorus, or potassium and whether or not lime is needed. Collect a soil sample to submit by digging clumps of soil from different areas of the garden, mixing them together, and submitting the sample for testing.

## How to Do a pH Test with a Kit

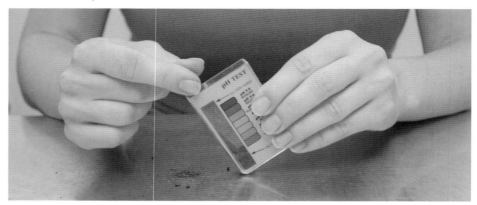

**1** Add soil to the kit from the area of the garden that you want to test. Then add water according to the instructions.

**2** Add the indicator powder to the water in the container; shake the container to mix the soil, water, and indicator powder.

**3** Hold the container against a piece of white paper so that you can check the color of the water with the soil in it against the color key on the container. The color of the water will match one of the colors in the key on the container. The reading will tell you whether the soil is acidic (low pH), alkaline (high pH), has low nitrogen levels, or has high phosphorus levels. After testing, you'll know what to add (or not add) to the soil.

## Adjust the Soil pH

The pH scale runs from 0 to 14. Most plants grow best in the range of 5.5 to 7.0, because nutrients in the soil are most available to plants at those soil pH levels. Landscape plants will usually struggle along if the soil pH is off, but edibles won't produce roots, leaves, and fruits for you to harvest if an off pH prevents them from getting the nutrients they need.

### pH Ranges for Common Edibles

| | | | | | |
|---|---|---|---|---|---|
| Asparagus | 6.0–8.0 | Cauliflower | 5.5–7.5 | Onion | 5.8–7.0 |
| Beet | 6.0–7.5 | Celery | 5.8–7.0 | Potato | 4.8–6.5 |
| Broccoli | 6.0–7.0 | Cucumber | 5.5–7.0 | Spinach | 6.0–7.5 |
| Cabbage | 6.0–7.5 | Lettuce | 6.0–7.0 | Tomato | 5.5–7.5 |
| Carrot | 5.5–7.0 | Muskmelon | 6.0–7.0 | | |

### How to Lower the pH

Soils with a pH below 5.5 are considered to be acidic. Soils with a pH above 7.0 are considered to be alkaline. To lower the pH of alkaline soils so that the pH is in the neutral range of 5.5 to 7.0, add aluminum sulfate according to package instructions. You can buy this at garden centers and home-improvement stores in the aisle with fertilizers and lawn care products. Some vegetables grow well with a lower pH, but most are happier with a higher pH. Blueberries and some fruit plants thrive in soils with a lower pH.

### How to Raise the pH

Spinach and plants in the cabbage family grow best in soils with a higher pH. You'll see that calcium is available to plants only at a higher pH. To raise the pH of the soil, add lime, which is also available at garden centers and home-improvement stores.

## Fertilizing Plants

Fertilizing is related to soil because you put the fertilizer in or on the soil, and the plants get the nutrients from fertilizers from the soil. Before fertilizing can be effective, the soil has to have the right properties to retain the nutrients from fertilizers and make them available to plants. If you've added compost, tested the pH, and adjusted it, and your plants still need more nutrients than those in the soil (and most edibles will), you can fertilize. More specifics on fertilizing materials, timing, and instructions are covered in Chapter 6.

# CHAPTER 5

# PLANTING YOUR GARDEN

The fun part of growing fruits and vegetables isn't testing the soil—it's picking out what to plant! But that can be the confusing part, too. Should you buy seeds or transplants? Container-grown or bare-root plants? What *is* a bare-root plant? How many of each plant should you buy? Should you get hybrids or heirlooms? Does it matter if the plants or seeds are organic? What about fruit trees? Should you buy trees grown in Oregon to plant in Delaware? Here's what you need to know in order to select the right plants and plant them in the right places for edible garden success.

## *Going Shopping*

Whether you're shopping for fruits or vegetables, you will have to choose between plants or seeds labeled "organic" and those that aren't. You'll choose between buying open-pollinated and hybrid selections, newer varieties and heirlooms. You can buy plants grown locally or plants shipped from far away. Before we even discuss varieties of plants, it's important to understand these broader categories and classifications and what they mean to your garden plans.

### Growing Organic

The term *organic*, when used as a label on something that is for sale, means that the product has been produced or grown according to a set of government standards. The simplest way to describe those standards is that they require growing without man-made chemicals. Is it better to buy organic seeds and transplants? That's a matter of preference. Plants grown organically usually have a lower impact on the environment, because the growers focus more on building the soil than spreading chemical fertilizers, use biological controls as opposed to synthetic (man-made) chemical controls, and work within the natural ecosystem rather than fighting it. At the end of the day, though, a big field of cabbage is not the same as a natural forest or prairie ecosystem.

### Open-Pollinated Varieties versus Hybrids

If you want to save seeds from year to year, you need to grow open-pollinated varieties. The words *heirloom* and *open-pollinated* are sometimes used interchangeably in gardening information, but they don't necessarily mean the same thing. *Heirloom* refers to a variety that was popular before World War II. *Open-pollinated* refers to a plant that produces stable characteristics from generation to generation. Heirlooms are usually, but not always, open-pollinated.

Seed packets will indicate whether the plant is a hybrid or heirloom.

Hybrids (F1 generation) are plants that grow from seeds produced by crossing two specific parent plants and saving the seeds. By crossing two plants, breeders can choose specific traits such as size, color, disease resistance, flavor, and more. Seeds from fruits of hybrid plants (F2 generation) can be saved and planted the next year, but they will not produce the same type of plants that they came from. When growing hybrids you sacrifice the ability to save seeds for next year for other perks like not losing your plants to a disease problem. The word "hybrid" does not mean that a plant is a GMO. There is nothing wrong with growing hybrids, unless you want to save seeds to plant next year.

### Locally Grown versus Ordered from Out of Town

You can order any plant you want online. There are some restrictions about shipping to certain states that limit what you can get, but those primarily apply to states with large acreages of commercial agriculture. However, just because you can order whatever you want from wherever you want doesn't mean you should.

Annual vegetables that you grow for one season can come from anywhere, and you're unlikely to have problems as long as the plants have been responsibly grown and cared for. Fruit trees and shrubs are a different matter. Plants grown for several years in the cool, moderate weather of the Pacific Northwest just won't be well adapted to the hot, humid weather of the Mid-Atlantic. When you buy fruits, ask where they were grown. Just because you're buying them at a local garden center does not mean they were locally grown. Try to source locally if you can.

### Buying the Healthiest Plants

You want to choose healthy plants that will take off and grow as soon as you plant them. You also want to purchase plants that have the best chance of staying healthy. Vegetables and fruits can have big problems with pests and diseases, but you can, in some cases, select plants that have resistance to pests or diseases. To avoid problems later, do your due diligence when picking.

### Signs That a Plant Is Healthy

**It's growing.** Look for new leaves at the end of stems and branches.

**It looks "in proportion" with its pot.** A healthy plant won't have roots growing out of the bottom of the pot, and it won't be spilling out of the pot.

**It has green leaves.** Unless the plant's leaves are supposed to be a different color (check the picture on the plant tag), its leaves should be a nice, medium green. Vegetables that have been sitting at the garden center for a long time start to turn yellow from lack of nutrients.

If a plant looks rotten, it is rotten. Don't buy it.

### Signs That a Plant Is Not Healthy

**The plant stems** are mushy and rotten.

**The tips of the branches** are dying. If a plant has a root problem, you can tell by looking at the ends of the branches. If the leaves are turning brown and dying, leave the plant at the garden center.

**The plant leaves are crispy,** the edges are brown and dry, or the plant is droopy, all of which mean the plant hasn't had enough water.

**The plants are overgrown**—growing out of the pot, falling over, and trailing along the shelves.

## Selecting for Disease Resistance

You can buy plants and seeds that have some level of resistance to common diseases affecting those types of plants. Look for these types of abbreviations on plant tags, labels, and catalog descriptions:

**BCMV:** Resistance to bean curly mosaic virus

**CMV:** Resistance to cucumber mosaic virus

**Foc, Foc 1:** Resistance to fusarium yellows

**PM:** Resistance to powdery mildew

**PVY:** Resistance to potato virus Y

**TMV:** Resistance to tobacco mosaic virus

**ToMV:** Resistance to tomato mosaic virus

**TSWV:** Resistance to tomato spotted wilt virus

**V:** Resistance to verticillium wilt

Those are some of the most common abbreviations for the most common diseases, but it's not an exhaustive list.

## *Planting the Vegetable Garden*

Some plants are easy to grow from seed, while others are easier if purchased as transplants. Whether you grow your own transplants or buy them, here's what you should plant outside as transplants and what you can grow from seed.

| Seeds | Transplants |
|-------|-------------|
| Bean | Basil |
| Carrot | Broccoli |
| Chives | Brussels sprouts |
| Cucumber | Cabbage |
| Dill | Cauliflower |
| Lettuce | Celery |
| Okra | Collards |
| Onion | Eggplant |
| Parsley | Kale |
| Parsnip | Leek |
| Pea | Pepper |
| Pumpkin | Spinach |
| Radish | Swiss chard |
| Turnip | Tomato |
| Watermelon | |

Some plants are best grown from transplants, including the broccoli being planted by this gardener.

## Starting Seeds Indoors

If you want to grow unusual varieties, you might have to order seeds and grow your own transplants. This isn't difficult, but it can be time-consuming. Look at the seed packets for information about when to start indoors. (You'll start seeds inside either a certain number of weeks before the last frost in spring or before the first frost in fall.)

**Supplies**

| | |
|---|---|
| Seed-starting mix | Heat mat |
| Seedling tray | Grow lights |
| Clear plastic cover | |

Fill tray with seed-sprouting mix, and plant seeds according to package instructions.

Purchase kits that have seedling flats and covers that fit, or use plastic wrap. Fill the seedling tray with moist seed-starting mix, not potting soil. (Place seed-starting mix in a bucket and moisten so that it is as damp as a moist sponge.) This lightweight mix is sterile and specially formulated to encourage easy, problem-free germination. Plant the seeds according to package instructions, and water the seeds in the soil, taking care not to wash them away. You don't have to use a heat mat, but using one will result in faster germination and growth.

Keep the seeds covered until they sprout, and then hang the grow lights 2 inches above the seedling tray. You don't have to use grow lights, but it is difficult to get strong seedlings without them. As the plants grow, move the lights up so that they are no more than 2 inches above the plants. Keep the seedling mix moist, but not

Cover seeds until they sprout.

soggy. Damping off (which looks like rotting or wilting of new seedlings) is a problem when seeds stay too wet and cold while germinating. When plants have three sets of leaves, you can transplant to a 4-inch pot.

## Planting Transplants Outdoors

Plant transplants outside according to the spacing the fully grown plants will need. Plant so that the soil line of the hole and the soil line of the transplant are even (except in special cases—see Growing Tip on the following page). Take the temperature of the soil to make sure it is warm enough. (The soil should be at least 60°F to 65°F for planting warm-weather vegetables such as tomatoes or peppers.) Before planting any transplants outside, prepare them by hardening them off.

---

**GROWING TIP**

Tomato plants and kale plants should be planted deep. Strip off all but the top two sets of leaves. Plant the entire rest of the plant below the soil line. Both of these plants will grow roots from the stem, making them stronger and healthier.

### Hardening Off before Planting Out

Vegetable transplants grown inside a greenhouse (or your house) need to be hardened off (acclimated to the change in temperature and light) before they're planted outside. Even if you buy plants that were sitting outside at a garden center, it's a good idea to harden them off before planting. For all you know, the plants were taken from the greenhouse, loaded on a truck, and brought to the garden center on the same day you saw them sitting outside.

### How to Harden Off Transplants

1. Place plants in a sheltered location such as a porch or patio for the day, and bring them in at night. Do this for three or four days.
2. Next, leave them outside all day and night in the protected location. Do this for about a week. Don't forget to water while you're doing this!
3. Finally, move the plants from the sheltered location (the porch or patio) to a more exposed location (the front sidewalk or driveway). Leave them there for three or four days.
4. Wait for a cloudy day (if possible) and plant your plants in the garden. Planting out on a cloudy day will lower the stress that the plants experience.

## Planting Seeds Outdoors

The key to success with seeds outdoors is to pay attention to them. Seeds have to stay moist while they are germinating. If they dry out, they will die—they have no reserves to draw on.

Harden off plants by setting them on your porch or patio during the day and bringing them in at night until they are acclimated to outside conditions.

### Take the Temperature

Before planting seeds outside, measure the temperature of the soil to make sure it is warm enough. Radishes, for example, need soil temperatures of 50°F or more.

Seedlings are fragile when they first sprout. Keep them moist but not soaking wet.

### Sow According to Finished Spacing and Germination Rates

Seed packets will have instructions to sow "thickly" (lettuce) or "thinly" (carrots, radishes). Usually these instructions correspond to germination rates. Radishes have a high germination rate, meaning that almost all of the seeds that you plant will sprout. Lettuce has a fairly high germination rate, but you want to grow lots of small leaf lettuce plants in a small space to encourage fast, leggy, tender growth. The more closely you can plant according to the finished spacing requirements, the fewer seeds you'll waste, and the less time you'll spend thinning.

### Cover with Seedling Mix

Seedling mix isn't just for indoor plants. It's my secret weapon for growing seeds outdoors. Instead of covering seeds with garden soil, cover them with seedling mix. This mix will stay loose and resist soil crusting, making it easier for the seeds to sprout.

### Check Seedlings and Water Frequently

Seeds need to stay moist but not soaking wet. Check them a couple of times a day. You might want to invest in a superfine hose nozzle to water without washing the seedlings away.

Further care for vegetables is discussed in Chapter 6.

## Planting the Fruit Garden

Fruits are a more permanent part of the garden and landscape. Once you plant an apple tree, you're not going to move it. Because of their long tenure in the garden, it is also important to plant fruit trees and shrubs correctly to avoid long-term problems. Before digging any holes, check the soil pH. Certain fruits, such as blueberries, are picky about the pH of the soil (they need acidic soil, or soil with a lower pH).

### Selecting Fruit Varieties

There are three main criteria to keep in mind when selecting fruit varieties:

1.  Chilling hours needed to produce fruit
2.  Height of mature tree or shrub
3.  Disease-resistance properties

In the individual profile pages for each fruit type, you will find recommendations for suitable varieties for gardens in the Mid-Atlantic.

### Planting Fruits

Before planting, test the soil pH, and adjust it if it is too high or too low.

Fruit plants can be purchased as container-grown or bare-root stock. Plant container-grown fruit trees and shrubs the same way you'd plant a landscape tree or shrub.

### How to Plant a Container-Grown Fruit Tree or Shrub

1.  Use a shovel or marking paint to mark the area for the hole. The planting hole should be two to three times as wide as the tree's rootball or container.
2.  Dig the planting hole. This hole should be just as deep as the rootball or container—no deeper! If you sharpen the spade before digging, this step will go faster.

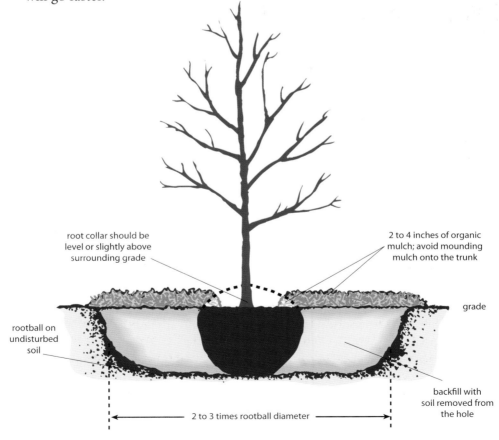

root collar should be level or slightly above surrounding grade

2 to 4 inches of organic mulch; avoid mounding mulch onto the trunk

grade

rootball on undisturbed soil

backfill with soil removed from the hole

2 to 3 times rootball diameter

**GROWING TIP**

Have you heard the saying, "Plant 'em high"? Well, that refers to trees. Trees will settle a bit after planting. Always make sure that you finish the job with the top of the tree's rootball about 3 inches above the soil line. If you plant a tree too deep, the place where the tree trunk and the tree roots meet can rot, which will kill the tree.

3. Set the tree in the planting hole to check the depth. If the top of the rootball or the soil level in the container is lower than the soil line around the edge of the planting hole, add some soil back into the hole, pull the tree out of the pot, and replace the tree in the hole. You never want the crown of the tree (the part where the tree trunk meets the tree roots) to be below the soil line.
4. Fill in around the tree with the same soil that you removed from the planting hole. Do not add fertilizer or new topsoil. Water will move more easily and the tree will root properly if the soil hole and around the planting hole is the same.
5. Mulch around the tree, taking care to pull the mulch away from the tree trunk. Do not create a mulch "volcano" around the tree (by piling mulch up high around the trunk)—that just encourages insects and creatures that snack on tree bark to take up residence next to your delicious young tree.
6. Water the tree. Plan to water newly planted trees every three days (every other day if it is hot and dry). New trees don't need to be staked unless they're in areas prone to heavy rains and frequent winds. It can take a couple of years for newly planted trees to root all the way into the surrounding soil, so continue to monitor your tree for signs that it needs water.

How to Plant a Bare-Root Fruit Tree or Shrub
1. Soak the bare roots in water the night before you plan to plant.
2. Dig a hole twice as wide as the diameter of the root spread and just as deep as the length of the roots.
3. Build a mound of soil in the center of the hole that is as high as the hole is deep.
4. Place the plant on top of the soil mound and spread the roots over the mound.
5. Fill in the soil around the plant, taking care that the point where the roots meet the trunk is above the soil line.
6. Finish by mulching around the plant.

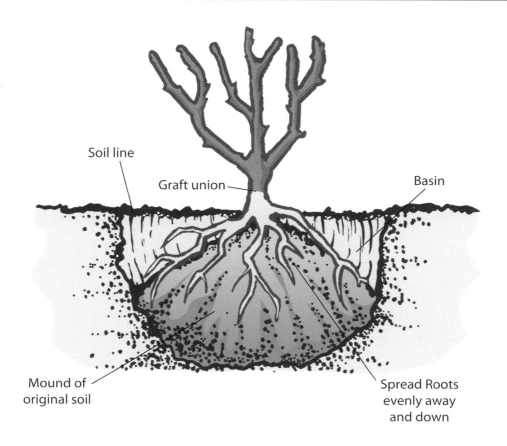

Soil line

Graft union

Basin

Mound of
original soil

Spread Roots
evenly away
and down

## *The Rest of the Garden*

Leave room in the vegetable garden for some flowers to attract pollinators.
In addition to planting flowers, you can let some of your early-season
vegetables bolt and flower. These flowers, blooming in early summer, will
attract pollinators to the first flowers on your vegetable plants.

The more diversity of plant life you have in the rest of your yard and
garden, the healthier your edibles will be. Other plants will support
beneficial insects and pollinators that contribute to the size and health of
your harvest.

# CHAPTER 6

# GROWING YOUR GARDEN

Once the soil is prepped, the plants are purchased, and the garden is planted, the heaviest lifting is done, until it's time to replant to accommodate a shift in seasons. Throughout the growing seasons, you'll need to keep your

plants producing prolifically by staying on top of these garden-maintenance tasks:

| | |
|---|---|
| thinning | staking |
| pinching | fertilizing |
| watering | controlling pests |
| weeding | harvesting |
| mulching | succession planting |

Mulching a vegetable garden with straw helps the soil retain moisture.

While the general principles of garden care apply to both fruits and vegetables, fruits have some unique issues and needs that are discussed further in Part II, preceding the individual plant profiles. You can take everything you learn from Part I, combine it with additional information about fruit trees from Part II, and successfully care for your fruit garden.

This garden was thinned when plants were smaller to allow for adequate space for the vegetables to grow and spread out.

## *Tools*

### CUTTING TOOLS

#### Hand pruners

**A** Hand pruners have a cutting blade and an anchor blade. They're good for pruning, harvesting vegetables, deadheading, and cutting bamboo stakes.

#### Snips

**B** Snips are a cross between scissors and hand pruners. They have a scissor-like cutting action, but they have a spring like hand pruners, for easy cutting. Snips are great for deadheading.

#### Scissors

**C** A good pair of scissors is a must for the garden. Use them to snip twine, deadhead, and harvest cut-and-come-again lettuce.

#### Velcro, twine, coated wire

**D** You always need something to tie a plant to a stake. Velcro and plastic-coated wire can be reused and work well with vegetables. Twine is invaluable because it is versatile. You can use it to create trellises for vining vegetables such as peas or cucumbers. Jute twine is the most commonly used type of garden twine, because it is strong.

### PLANT STAKES AND SUPPORT

You can use anything long and narrow to stake plants. When you go to buy stakes, you'll run into a few common types. Here's more about each of the stakes and support pictured on page 53.

*From left to right:*

**Metal or plastic-coated metal stake**

**A** These heavy-duty stakes are perfect for vegetable gardening. They won't break as plants get tall and heavy.

**Natural or dyed bamboo stake**

**B** The light color of natural bamboo stakes makes them stand out more against dark green garden foliage, while the dyed-green stakes blend in. Bamboo stakes are easy to cut to size with hand pruners. They are best used for vegetables that stay fairly small. You can also use them to make a latticework for peas to climb up.

**Wood stake**

**C** Thicker wood stakes come in handy for staking peppers. Most people don't think of staking peppers, but they will grow taller and produce more fruit if they have some support.

**Tomato spiral stake**

**D** For use with tomatoes, which can twine around the spiral for support.

**Tomato cage support**

**E** Tomato cages are made of aluminum and provide support for tomatoes, peppers, eggplants, tomatillos, and any large vegetables.

---

## DIGGING TOOLS

**Hand hoe**

**A** The scary-looking hand hoe actually makes planting easier and faster. This is a hoe with a sharp blade and a short handle. Use it as you would use a pickax to quickly plant vegetable transplants.

**Trowel**

**B** Trowels are small shovels used for weeding and planting. You can buy trowels made of plastic or made with metal blades and wood handles.

### Soil knife

**C** Soil knives are indispensable. One side of the blade is sharpened, and the other is serrated like a saw. Use these to plant transplants, dig up weeds, and cut through roots. Some soil knives have depth measurements marked on them, which helps with planting. A soil knife is really a more useful version of a trowel.

### Shovel (not pictured)

Shovels have long, straight wood handles and curved or straight bottoms. Use shovels to dig up plants, dig planting holes for trees and shrubs, and move compost or soil.

### Hoe

**D** There are many different types of hoes. Hoes with narrow ends are excellent for digging planting rows. Hoes with larger, wider ends are helpful for spreading soil and mulching.

---

## RAKING AND SPREADING TOOLS

### Four-tine claw

**A** A four-tine claw has a long wood handle and a metal top with four curved tines. (This tool is sometimes called a cultivator.) Use a four-tine claw to cultivate and dig between vegetable garden rows, rake mulch in narrow garden beds, and incorporate compost and soil amendments into the garden.

### Hard rake

**B** A hard rake is a cross between a leaf rake and a four-tine claw. It has hard metal prongs like a claw, but a wider head like a leaf rake. Use this to rake soil and spread mulch. Hard rakes are also useful for spreading gravel and raking mulch pathways.

### Garden fork or pitchforks

**C** Pitchforks have long, straight handles and scooped heads similar to those of shovels, but they have sharpened tines instead of solid metal blades. Use pitchforks to turn the compost pile and move mulch around. Garden forks have handles like spades—with a grip you can put your hand through on the end—but they have flat tines that are wider than pitchfork tines. Use garden forks to divide plants and turn over weeds.

## WATERING TOOLS

### Garden hose

**A** The garden hose is your main tool for watering plants. It's worth the money to buy a good 50-foot, heavy-duty, no-kink hose. You'll be glad you made the extra investment.

**A**

### Soaker hose

**B** Soaker hoses are porous hoses that you connect to a faucet, place in the garden, and leave there. When you turn on the faucet, water slowly seeps out of the hose, reaching the plants where they need it most—their roots. Use soaker hoses if you don't have the time or money to create drip irrigation systems. Soaker hoses come in handy during short periods of hot, dry weather, because they're easy to move around. You can also get sprinkler timers to put on the ends of soaker hoses to create your own DIY irrigation system that will turn on and off while you're out of town. Tomatoes, especially, benefit from soaker hoses, because tomatoes crack or get blossom-end rot during periods of wet/dry/wet/dry watering.

**B**

### Watering wand

**C** Every gardener needs a watering wand. This is a long tube with a water breaker on the end that disperses the water pressure from the hose. Watering wands make it easy for you to water near the base of a plant without bending over, and to reach across rows.

**C**

### Water breaker

**D** Water breakers can be used with watering wands or on the ends of hoses. Sometimes called rosettes, water breakers disperse the flow of water so that it is gentler and less likely to cause soil to splatter. Water breakers should be used when you hand-water plants. They're especially good for watering newly planted plants and seedlings.

**D**

These carrot seedlings will need to be thinned to leave at least 3 inches between plants in order to harvest larger carrots later.

# Garden Maintenance Activities

Calling these activities "tasks" or "chores" makes them sound a lot more difficult and time-consuming than they really are. The largest amount of work in vegetable gardening is getting the garden planted. The rest of it can be done in an hour or two after work or on the weekends.

### Thinning

When you plant seeds, you usually plant more than you'll need if they all sprout. That leads to thinning, or removing some of the plants in the row to open up space for the plants you leave to grow. Save yourself work by sowing seeds with good germination rates fairly thinly and according to the recommended final spacing for the plants. If you don't thin root vegetables such as radishes, carrots, turnips, beets, and so forth, you'll end up with a lot of small roots instead of the fat, juicy roots you want.

Thinning is my least-favorite garden chore, and sometimes I don't do it. That has worked out fine for carrots, but not so well for radishes. To thin without disturbing the other plants, use scissors to snip the seedling off at the soil level.

## Pinching

You can pinch plants such as tomatoes and peppers to get fewer, larger fruits. Pinching tomatoes also helps prevent these vigorous plants from putting energy into leaves rather than fruits. You can pinch the side shoots that grow directly between the tomato's main stem and the productive branches. You can also let these shoots grow from the main stem and pinch them after they have one set of leaves.

Pinching tomato suckers (the sprouts between the leaves and the stem) will lead to fewer, larger tomatoes being produced.

## Watering

Watering is probably the most important technique to master in edible gardening. Vegetables and fruits only produce well if they are happy and not stressed. If they receive too much water, not enough water, or inconsistent water, they become stressed and can be afflicted by pests, diseases, and physiological problems. You can water vegetables by hand or by using irrigation.

### Watering Seedlings

Seeds and seedlings need to stay continually moist while sprouting. They don't have reserves to fall back on. If you plant seeds in the garden, check them at least twice a day to make sure they are staying moist.

### Watering by Hand

Hand-watering is a good thing to do if you want to relax at the end of the day or spend some time outside before going to work. Water by holding the hose nozzle at the base of each plant and counting to five.

---

**GROWING TIP**

Before you head into the house after work, or before you get in the car to go to work, do a lap around your garden. Water any plants that need to be watered, and keep an eye out for pests or anything amiss. If you set a time to do this, you won't let garden maintenance get ahead of you, and you'll give your plants the best care. (Plus, it's fun!)

### Watering with Irrigation

Using irrigation or soaker hoses isn't a "fix it and forget it" option. You still have to monitor the plants to see if they need water and turn on the irrigation or set the timer. It's better to water all plants as deeply as possible and as infrequently as possible without stressing them. Don't let the irrigation run for five minutes, five times a day. Set it up to give the plants enough water to soak the top inch of soil. When that's dry, water again.

Watering wand

Lay a soaker hose after you plant, while the plants are still small. Use sod staples to hold the hose in place.

## Weeding

Weeding is a constant battle, but by staying on top of it continuously, you can lessen the problems you have with weeds over time.

There are a few ways to deal with weeds:

- Use a pre-emergent herbicide to prevent weed seeds from sprouting. (This does not work on perennial weeds.)
- Hand-pull or dig weeds with large taproots (such as dandelions).
- Turn over the soil or rake under small weeds. (This works best for annual weeds.)
- Use herbicide to kill the weeds.

### Why Bother to Remove Weeds?

Weeds are unsightly, for one thing, but they also take sunlight, nutrients, and water from the plants you want to grow. It's worth it to remove them.

## WHAT IS A WEED, AND WHAT IS A SEEDLING

Sometimes seedlings look like weeds. In this picture, you can see nasturtium seedlings (light green circular leaves) sprouting along the edges of the raised-bed box. In the center of the photo, next to the lettuce, are dollarweed plants (dark green circular leaves growing flat in the raised bed), which look like nasturtiums. Know what you're removing before you remove it!

Dollar weed masquerading as nasturtium seedlings.

### WEED TYPES

The following weed types are not "official" distinctions but rather categories of weeds you'll have to deal with. Here are the characteristics of certain types of weeds and how you deal with them.

### Annual

Annual weeds complete their life cycle during one season by growing, flowering, and setting seeds. The main objective in preventing annual weeds from spreading is to prevent them from flowering. You can mow or cut these weeds frequently, pull them out, or use herbicide to kill them. Pre-emergent herbicide works well on annual weeds.

### Perennial and Biennial Clumping

Perennial clumping weeds come back every year. Biennial weeds grow a large plant with a taproot one year and then flower and set seeds the next year. Both types will eventually flower and set seeds, which establishes new clumps. These types of weeds respond well to hand-digging, because they do not have runners or stems that can break off and start new plants.

### Perennial Spreading

Perennial spreading weeds are the most difficult to control. These weeds are most easily eradicated with systemic herbicides, which are weedkillers that are absorbed by the plant and kill the plant from the inside. You can also kill these weeds by hand-digging them up.

Wood mulch in a vegetable garden

## Mulching

Mulching the vegetable garden will save you a lot of time watering and weeding. It is amazing the difference that a thick, 3-inch layer of mulch will make. If you mow your own lawn and don't use chemicals on it, save the grass clippings—they make great mulch, and they add nutrients to the soil.

Other good materials for vegetable garden mulch include:

| | |
|---|---|
| Shredded newspaper | Compost |
| Shredded bark mulch | Wheat straw |
| Aged manure | Shredded leaves |

There's a misconception that you shouldn't use wood mulch in a vegetable garden. Now, you wouldn't want to use treated wood mulch or sawdust, but shredded hardwood mulch is more beneficial than detrimental. If you can buy shredded hardwood mulch with compost in it, even better!

When mulching around your plants, avoid mounding the mulch up around the stems of the plants, which can cause the plants to rot.

## Staking

You'll stake certain vegetables to let them grow upright and reach the light. You'll stake other vegetables because their brittle stems can't support the weight of their fruits.

## Vegetables That Need Trellises

Certain vegetables will grow up trellises (wood, metal, or string). Certain plants need to have trellises to grow.

## Vegetables That Can Grow up Trellises

Cucumber
Pumpkin
Squash

## Vegetables That Must Grow up Trellises or Lattices

Garden pea
Pole bean

## Vegetables That Need Stakes or Cages

Eggplant
Okra
Pepper
Tomato

**A word from experience:** It is much easier to place the plant supports before (trellises) or right after (everything else) planting than it is to try to wrestle a large, viny plant into a cage or support after it has started growing.

## *Fertilizing*

Vegetables and fruits need to be routinely fed (fertilized) in order to produce food for us to eat. Different plants have different requirements, which are listed in the individual plant profiles. Using bloodmeal and compost, along with other organic fertilizers will improve the soil while feeding the plants. When possible, use organic fertilizers. Your garden will benefit from this in the long run. Think of synthetic fertilizer as a candy bar for the garden. It gives quick nutrients to the plants, but the effects are fleeting. Synthetic fertilizer doesn't benefit the garden over time. Fertilizers all have a combination of nutrients in them. Most of them have the "Big Three" macronutrients: nitrogen (N), phosphorus (P),

I always stake my peas by making latticeworks with sticks that fall out of the trees in the yard over the winter.

When tying a plant to a stake, line the stake up to the main stem of the plant. Then tie the plant to the stake, but never tie the string so tight that the plant is smashed against the stake.

Sidedress plants with organic fertilizers (sprinkle them on the soil alongside the plants) every few weeks to keep your vegetables growing.

and potassium (K). Some fertilizers have micronutrients such as calcium, magnesium, manganese, and iron. Fertilizer labels include what is called an "analysis," which is the percentage of each nutrient contained in the product.

### DIFFERENT TYPES OF FERTILIZER

You might have grown up with Miracle-Gro, a common brand-name synthetic fertilizer, but you have other choices.

### Organic or Natural Liquid Fertilizer

Organic or natural liquid fertilizers are usually made from kelp, fish emulsion, or a combination of each. Mix this type of fertilizer with water in watering cans to water into the soil. Some organic or natural liquid fertilizers are used as foliar feeds (diluted and sprayed on the leaves). Mix these fertilizers with water in a pressurized sprayer, and spray the leaves of the plants. The plants will soak up the nutrients through their leaves. Some organic fertilizers are smelly, so don't use them right before you have an outdoor barbecue. Organic fertilizers tend to have more micronutrients along with the "Big Three." These fertilizers will build your soil health over time.

### Conventional or Synthetic Liquid Fertilizer

Synthetic liquid fertilizers have nitrogen, phosphorus, and potassium in them in one combination or another. These fertilizers are formulated for different types of plants. You can buy houseplant fertilizers, fertilizers for acid-loving plants, vegetable fertilizers, and fertilizers formulated to encourage more blooms on plants. You can buy conventional fertilizer in concentrated liquid or concentrated powder forms. In both cases, you need to mix the concentrate with water. Some brands of fertilizer have special attachments that will do the mixing for you. Synthetic fertilizers usually just have macronutrients: nitrogen, phosphorus, and potassium. They will not build soil health over time.

### Granular Fertilizer

Granular fertilizer is sometimes called slow-release fertilizer. They're really two different things. Granular fertilizer is pelletized. Some granulars are quick-release and break down immediately. Some granular fertilizers have a mixture of quick and slow-release fertilizers. Sometimes granular fertilizer is combined with pre-emergent weed control in a "weed and feed" product. Don't use weed and feed products where you've just planted seeds, or they won't sprout.

### Organic Non-Liquid Fertilizer

Blood meal, bone meal, and fish emulsion are organic or natural fertilizers made from different mixtures of natural, or non-synthetic, ingredients. Usually you will sidedress or mix these fertilizers into the soil. They break down over time and feed the microorganisms in the soil as much as the plants. If you want to build up the fertility of the soil, natural fertilizers are better to use than a quick shot of synthetic fertilizer.

### Nutrient Deficiencies

If your plant leaves are turning weird colors (purple, yellow), they might have nutrient deficiencies. Nutrient deficiencies cause highly predictable results, and it's usually possible to diagnose whether a nutrient deficiency is a problem by looking at the plant.

The diagram below shows the symptoms caused by the most common nutrient deficiencies.

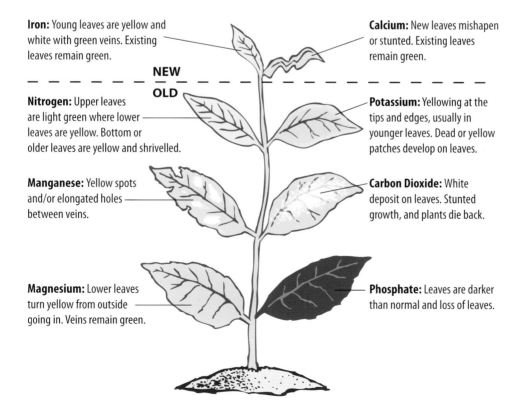

**Iron:** Young leaves are yellow and white with green veins. Existing leaves remain green.

**Calcium:** New leaves mishapen or stunted. Existing leaves remain green.

**NEW**

**OLD**

**Nitrogen:** Upper leaves are light green where lower leaves are yellow. Bottom or older leaves are yellow and shrivelled.

**Potassium:** Yellowing at the tips and edges, usually in younger leaves. Dead or yellow patches develop on leaves.

**Manganese:** Yellow spots and/or elongated holes between veins.

**Carbon Dioxide:** White deposit on leaves. Stunted growth, and plants die back.

**Magnesium:** Lower leaves turn yellow from outside going in. Veins remain green.

**Phosphate:** Leaves are darker than normal and loss of leaves.

If you see nutrient deficiency problems in your plants, test the soil pH. If the pH is too high or too low, it won't matter if you fertilize— the plants won't be able to get the nutrients from the soil.

## Controlling Pests

There is nothing more discouraging than carefully tending your garden only to see it being chewed apart by pests. Each type of edible has its own pest problems, which are outlined in the individual plant profiles. There is also a chart of pests and diseases beginning on page 67 to help you identify what the problem is and how to fix it. Before you take action, it's important to understand pests, pesticides, and their relationship to your garden.

### Pests: A Fact of Life

There are insects and bacteria and fungi everywhere, eating everything, including each other. On a single tree in the forest, there could be four hundred types of caterpillars, four hundred types of insects eating the caterpillars, and thousands of bacterial organisms eating the insects. What this means is that ecosystems have their own checks and balances. When we use chemicals to control certain pests, we are messing with the checks and balances, and that can have consequences.

### Diversity and Pest Problems

I hardly ever have to use pesticides in my garden, primarily because I have a high tolerance for pest activity, and I also grow a lot of different types of fruits, vegetables, flowers, trees, and shrubs in my yard. When you grow a biologically diverse garden and have a biologically diverse landscape, you support the beneficial insects that prey on harmful insects.

The way you lay out the vegetable garden matters in terms of pest control, too. If you plant all of your eggplants in one spot, and all of your tomatoes in another spot, and all of your beans in another spot, you are giving pests an all-you-can-eat buffet they can enjoy without having to leave their chairs. Try planting clumps of each edible throughout the garden. The pests might find one clump and stick with it, allowing the other plants to thrive.

## Beneficial Insects

You can encourage beneficial insects, such as ladybugs, lacewings, soldier beetles, wasps, and others, to live in your yard by limiting the use of broad-spectrum (kills everything) chemicals and by growing a diverse landscape. Remember, chemicals that kill everything kill the insects that are working for you, too.

## Integrated Pest Management

If you're serious about growing all of your own food and you can find the time, I highly recommend taking pesticide training at your county extension service. Not only will you learn how to safely apply pesticides, but you'll learn about integrated pest management, or IPM. There are four pillars of IPM:

**Set action thresholds:** You don't have to spray at the first sight of an insect. Decide what amount of damage you're willing to live with.

**Monitor and identify pests:** Early detection leads to early action before much damage can be done.

**Prevention:** Do what you can to prevent pest and disease problems. Plant resistant varieties, use barriers to keep pests from reaching the plants, and provide plants with the best care possible so that they can withstand pest problems.

**Control:** After all of the other steps, you can decide how to control the pests. Controls can be organic or synthetic, involve treating the pests or pulling out the affected plants.

### Organic versus Synthetic Controls

There's a misconception that if you use an organic pesticide, you're not putting yourself or your plants in any danger. That is false. There are organic pesticides made from naturally occurring ingredients that are just as deadly as pesticides that are made in a lab. When deciding to use a pesticide to control weeds, pests, or diseases, always read the label and follow the instructions for dosage, protective equipment, reentry timing, and harvest windows.

### Controlling Mammalian Pests

Deer, rabbits, chipmunks, and squirrels are all problems in the edible garden. The most effective way to control these pests is with barriers. Fencing, repellents, and netting are just about the only way to keep these pests out of the garden. If you're growing vegetables in rows, think about using row covers to keep pests away.

For more information about individual pests, see the chart beginning on page 67.

## Harvesting

You've prepared the soil, planted the plants, fertilized them, tended them, and kept other creatures from eating them. It's time to harvest! But *when* do you harvest?

It's easier to tell when some fruits and vegetables are ready than others. Information about harvesting each plant type is found in the individual plant profiles.

Here are some general tips about harvesting:

- Let fruits and vegetables that you want to be sweet ripen on the vine or plant for as long as possible. If you pick a tomato green, it will turn red and soften, but it won't be as tasty.
- Use hand pruners or scissors to harvest eggplants, peppers, and other fruits that don't easily snap off. You don't want to yank the plant out of the ground.
- Harvest in the morning—that's when everything has the highest water content, which means it will last longer before eating and will be fresher and crispier.
- Learn how big the finished product is supposed to be, so that you know when to harvest. If the eggplant is supposed to be 1 inch wide and 4 inches long, and you let it grow to be 4 inches wide and 1 foot long, it will not taste good.

Some vegetables are easier to harvest with scissors, so you don't yank the plant out of the ground. Here, the gardener is using scissors to cut the pepper. If she twisted the pepper off the plant, she could break or damage the rest of the plant.

## Troubleshooting

| Plant | Pest Problem | Symptoms | Solution |
|---|---|---|---|
| **Apple** | Apple scab | Hard scabby growth on apple fruits and on leaves | Plant resistant varieties, use fungicides according to label |
| | Cedar apple rust | Yellow spots with red rings on leaves | Remove junipers and crabapples, plant resistant varieties, prune off galls from junipers and cedars |
| | Fire blight | Wilting and dried up tips and leaves | Cut off infected parts and throw away, plant resistant varieties |
| | Codling moth | Holes in fruits | Pheremone traps, hygiene (pick up fallen fruits), insecticides |
| **Arugula** | Flea beetles | Presence of insects | Use row covers directly after seeds have sprouted or seedlings have been planted |
| **Basil** | Snails and slugs | Holes in leaves | Diatomaceous earth |
| **Bay** | No pest problems | | |
| **Bean** | Thrips and aphids | Presence of insects, dry spots on leaves | Insecticidal soap |
| | Bean beetle, corn earworms | Presence of insects | Row covers after planting, insecticides labeled for specific pests |
| **Beets** | Downy mildew, leaf spot | Grey-white fuzz | Fungicides (treatment not usually necessary) |
| **Blackberry** | Birds | Fruits half-eaten | Netting |
| | Crown borers | Wilting of new growth | Cut off affected area below the wilting point |
| **Blueberry** | Birds | Disappearing fruit | Netting |
| | Cranberry fruitworm | Nets in the shrubs | Cut off affected area and throw away |
| **Broccoli** | Cabbage looper | Moths flying around at night, holes in the leaves, presence of caterpillars | *Bacillus thuringiensis (B.t.)* |
| **Brussels Sprouts** | Aphids | Presence of insects, sticky honeydew produced by ants farming the aphids | Blast with water, use insecticidal soap |
| | Cabbage loopers, cabbage worm | Presence of insects, holes in the leaves | *Bacillus thuringiensis (B.t.)* |
| **Cabbage** | Cabbage loopers, cabbage worm | Presence of insects, holes in the leaves | *Bacillus thuringiensis (B.t.)* |
| | Black rot | Black tips on leaves, brown patches | Plant resistant varieties |
| | Flea beetles | Presence of insects | Row covers after planting |
| **Carrot** | Parsley worm (black swallowtail caterpillars) | Presence of insects | Control not usually necessary |
| **Cauliflower** | Slugs and snails | Presence of slugs, holes in the leaves | Diatomaceous earth |
| | Cabbage root maggots | Wilting plant | Row covers immediately after transplanting |
| **Chives** | No pest problems | | |
| **Cilantro/ Coriander** | Aphids | Presence of insects, sticky honeydew on plants | Blast with water, use insecticidal soap |
| | Whiteflies | Presence of tiny white insects | Sticky traps |
| **Citrus** | Scale | Presence of small, black insects (look like ticks), mildew around scale | Keep the plant outside in stress-free conditions |
| **Collards** | Aphids | Presence of insects, sticky honeydew on plants | Blast with water, use insecticidal soap |
| | Cabbage worm, cabbage looper | Presence of insects, holes in the leaves | Row covers after transplanting |

(continued on page 68)

## Troubleshooting (continued)

| Plant | Pest Problem | Symptoms | Solution |
|---|---|---|---|
| **Corn** | Birds | Tops of ears ripped apart | Netting |
| | Armyworm, corn earworm | Holes on the plants | *Bacillus thuringiensis* (B.t.) |
| **Cucumber** | Cucumber beetles | Presence of insects | Floating row covers |
| | Squash vine borer | Sudden wilting of plants | Floating row covers (nothing you can do once they strike) |
| **Dill** | Tomato hornworms | Presence of worms, entire plant defoliated | Handpick and destroy |
| **Eggplant** | Tomato hornworms | Presence of worms, entire plant defoliated | Handpick and destroy |
| | Colorado potato beetle | Orange eggs on underside of leaves, insects present | Crush eggs, use row covers after planting |
| **Fennel** | Black swallowtail caterpillars | Caterpillars present | Control not necessary |
| **Fig** | Root knot nematode | Test soil before planting | Plant resistant varieties |
| | A variety of blights | Off-color leaves | Plant resist varieties, prune to allow air movement within tree |
| **Garlic** | No pest problems | | |
| **Grape** | Fungal diseases | Spots on leaves, mildew on fruit | Prune to promote good air circulation |
| **Hardy Kiwi** | Root knot nematodes | Test soil before planting | Fumigate soil prior to planting if nematodes are present |
| **Kale** | Aphids | Presence of insects | Blast with water, use insecticidal soap |
| | Cabbage worms | Holes in leaves, presence of insects | *Bacillus thuringiensis* (B.t.) |
| **Kohlrabi** | Flea beetles, cabbage worms | Holes in leaves | Floating row covers |
| **Leeks** | No pest problems | | |
| **Lettuce** | Aphids | Presence of insects | Blast with water |
| **Loquat** | Fungal diseases | Black spots on leaves and fruit | Fungicides |
| **Marjoram** | Aphids and spider mites | Presence of insects | Keep plant stress free, water in times of drought |
| **Melon** | Cucumber beetles | Presence of insects | Floating row covers |
| | Squash vine borer | Sudden wilting of plants | Floating row covers (nothing you can do once they strike) |
| **Mint** | No pest problems | | |
| **Okra** | No pest problems | | |
| **Onions** | Onion root maggots | Wilting tops | Diatomaceous earth |
| **Parsley** | Black swallowtail caterpillars | Presence of insects, chewed-on plants | Do not control. They will go away. |
| **Parsnip** | Black swallowtail caterpillars | Presence of insects, chewed-on plants | Do not control. They will go away. |
| **Peach and Nectarine** | Plum curculio | Sticky sap coming out of fruits | Insecticides applied at petal fall of flowers |
| | Numerous other diseases | Various | Consult local cooperative extension for a spray plan |
| **Pear** | Fireblight | Ends of branches look burned | Plant resistant varieties |
| | Pear psylla | Presence of insects, brown spots on leaves | Dormant oil during winter |

## Troubleshooting (continued)

| Plant | Pest Problem | Symptoms | Solution |
|---|---|---|---|
| Pea | Aphids | Presence of insects | Spray with water |
| Pecan | | | Pest control not practical, plant varieties recommended for Mid-Atlantic |
| Pepper | Viruses | Off-colored leaves, wilting | Plant resistant varieties |
| Persimmon | Few pest problems | | |
| Plum | Plum curculio | Sticky sap coming out of fruits | Insecticides applied at petal fall of flowers |
| | Brown rot | Yellow growths on plum, shriveled appearance | Fungicides |
| | Black knot | Warty growths on branches | Cut off affected and dispose of branches |
| Radish | No pest problems | | |
| Rosemary | Mealybugs and scale | Whitish downy fungus on plant, black spots on plant | Horticultural oil |
| Sage | Spider mites | Red dots on leaves | Blast with water, give the plant extra water |
| Spinach | Leaf miners | Brown trails and dried sections of leaves | Floating row covers after planting |
| | Fungal problems | Rotten leaves | Keep water off leaves |
| Strawberry | Botrytis | Moldy fruits, flowers | Fungicides |
| | Birds | Holes in fruits | Nets |
| Summer Squash | Cucumber beetles | Presence of insects | Floating row covers |
| | Squash vine borer | Sudden wilting of plants | Floating row covers (nothing you can do once they strike) |
| Sweet Potato | Sweet potato weevil | Tunnels under the skin | Plant resistant varieties |
| Swiss Chard | Aphids, leaf miners | Presence of insects, dried spots on leaves | Blast with water, use insecticidal soap |
| Tarragon | No pest problems | | |
| Thyme | Aphids and spider mites | Presence of insects | Blast with water, give extra water |
| | Fungal problems | Rotten leaves and stems | Stop watering |
| Tomatillo | Cutworms | Dead seedlings | Wrap bottom 3 inches of stem in newspapwer |
| | Tomato hornworms | Presence of worms, defoliated plants | Handpick and destroy |
| Tomato | Tomato hornworms | Presence of worms, defoliated plants | Handpick and destroy |
| | Various viruses | Discolored leaves, wilting plants | Start by planting resistant varieties |
| Turnip | Root maggots | Wilting tops | Row covers to keep adults from laying eggs |
| Winter Squash | Cucumber beetles | Presence of insects | Floating row covers |
| | Squash vine borer | Sudden wilting of plants | Floating row covers (nothing you can do once they strike) |

# PART II

# FRUIT & VEGETABLE PROFILES

By now, you've clued into the fact that this book is organized a bit differently than many books about edible gardening. It isn't a straight alphabetical list. It isn't organized entirely by type. To make it easier to grow these edibles, the book is organized around the way these plants grow—where they grow in the garden and which season you plant and harvest.

First is a discussion of the fruits, organized by plant type: fruit and nut trees, shrubs and brambles, and vining and "garden" fruits. The size and type of fruits determines where you plant them, when you harvest them, and which varieties will work best for your garden.

Blueberries forming on three-year-old blueberry shrubs.

## Botanical Names and Common Names

All plants (all living things) have a scientific name composed of a genus (first word) and species (second word). Those names are standard throughout the world. The scientific names of plants are also referred to as botanical names, and the language of them is known as botanical Latin.

*Solanum lycopersicum* is the botanical name for tomato. The botanical name is always italicized. Cultivars of tomato include 'Brandywine' and 'Cherokee Purple', among others. Cultivars are always unitalicized and in single quotes.

Because different cultivars or varieties grow well under different circumstances, it's important to do your research before shopping. We've included recommended varieties or cultivars in the individual plant profiles.

In a few cases, mostly with fruit plants, there are several species of a fruit within one genus. Some species grow better in the Mid-Atlantic than others. Blueberries are one example of this. That is also noted in individual plant descriptions.

Next up are the vegetables and herbs, organized by cool and warm season. In the Mid-Atlantic, the most influential factor governing vegetable and herb growing is the season. Certain plants will grow only during the cool season, and others during the warm season. Still others confound us by tolerating both seasons equally well.

While fruit trees and shrubs are a permanent fixture in the landscape, and thus have to be selected and planted accordingly, most vegetables and herbs are grown as annuals and can and should be moved around. Fruit tree care centers on growth for longevity, while vegetable care is oriented toward getting the biggest harvest for one season.

At the beginning of each section, there's information pertinent to planting just those types of (or seasonal) plants. Ideally, you can take the book to the garden center or home-improvement store, get what you need to grow a garden for the season at hand, go home, plant, and start growing.

Planting flowers around your vegetable garden will add color and attract pollinators.

## Find Your Favorites

You can check the index at the back of the book, but you can also use the alphabetical list below to find your favorite edibles.

Apple, 88
Arugula, 134
Asparagus, 136
Basil, 220
Bean, 190
Beet, 138
Blackberry, 114
Blueberry, 110
Broccoli, 140
Brussels sprouts, 142
Cabbage, 144
Carrot, 146
Cauliflower, 148
Cherry, 94
Chestnut, 96
Chives, 222
Cilantro/Coriander, 178
Collards, 150
Corn, 194
Cucumber, 196
Dill, 180

Eggplant, 198
Fennel, 182
Fig, 112
Garlic, 152
Grape, 120
Kale, 154
Kohlrabi, 156
Leek, 158
Lettuce, 160
Marjoram, 224
Melon, 122
Mint, 226
Nectarine, 98
Okra, 200
Onion, 162
Oregano, 228
Parsley, 184
Parsnip, 164
Pea, 166
Peach, 98
Pear, 100

Pecan, 102
Pepper, 202
Persimmon, 104
Plum, 106
Potato, 206
Radish, 168
Raspberry, 114
Rhubarb, 124
Rosemary, 230
Sage, 232
Spinach, 170
Strawberry, 126
Summer squash, 208
Swiss chard, 172
Tarragon, 234
Thyme, 236
Tomatillo, 210
Tomato, 212
Turnip, 174
Winter squash, 216

# CHAPTER 7

# FRUIT & NUT GARDENING

Planting a fruit tree or shrub is like making an investment in the garden. It can take as many as ten years to get a harvest from a nut tree. Most fruit trees bear (produce) fruit somewhere between two and six years after planting. When you buy fruits, the source (website, catalog, garden center) should be able to tell you when the tree will bear. By the time you buy some plants (citrus, particularly), they're already of bearing age, and you won't have to wait.

Peach trees laden with fruit

## *Choosing Fruits and Nuts*

First things first: nut trees are fruit trees. Nuts are the fruits of the trees that bear them, just like a zucchini squash is the fruit of a zucchini plant, and a tomato is the fruit of a tomato plant. Fruit trees and nut trees are both, from this point forward, referred to as "fruit trees." The diagrams, care instructions, and other general information in this section that refers to "fruit trees" is also applicable to nut trees, unless otherwise noted.

Fruit trees and shrubs (and vines, for that matter) take up a lot of space in the garden relative to vegetable and herb plants, and they're more permanent. It's important to choose plants that produce fruits that you like to eat and to be mindful of space. Most fruit trees need full sun in order to produce well. If you're starting with a blank slate of a landscape, the sky can be the limit. If you are trying to work fruits into an existing landscape, siting is trickier.

There are many factors that influence which fruit plants you choose for your garden. When selecting fruits to grow at home, you'll need to pay attention to these characteristics:

Source
Tree size
Rootstock
Bloom time
Pollination requirements
Pest and disease resistance
Chilling hours required
Cold hardiness
What you like to eat
Whether you'll eat everything fresh or preserve part of your harvest

One is not more important than the other. All of the above characteristics influence how a fruit plant grows and whether you'll be successful growing it.

### Source

Thoughtfully selecting the source of fruit plants is essential to successful fruit growing. You'll have more long-term success if you purchase locally grown fruit plants than if you purchase plants grown in greenhouses or fields on the other side of the country. Different weather conditions, different pests, and different diseases affect fruit trees much more than plants such as tomatoes or green beans that live for one season and then are replanted.

Pecans, blueberries, apples, and peaches are all types of fruit plants that should be acquired from local sources due to various problems with pest and disease resistance. If you purchase online, these plants should be labeled for growing specifically in the Mid-Atlantic. Just because a plant is hardy in a particular growing zone doesn't mean that it will be well suited to growing in your area. There's much more to think about with fruits than cold tolerance.

## Plant Size

The largest fruit plants that you can grow are nut trees. Apples follow close behind. Plums, pears, and peaches are the next smallest (in that order). Vining fruits such as grapes are about equal with shrubby fruits such as blackberries and blueberries in terms of space requirements. Melons and strawberries take up a lot of space but can be easily moved from year to year. Before buying a particular fruit, decide whether you truly have the space for its eventual size and if you want to commit that space over a period of ten to twenty years.

## Rootstock

The ultimate size of many fruit plants depends on the rootstock. Most fruit trees have two parts. The top of the plant, which produces the fruit that we eat, is called the scion. Rather than growing from seed, scions are cuttings from other plants of the same variety. (This process was the original "cloning.") The bottom of the plant is called the rootstock. Rootstocks can cause a scion to grow more slowly, increase cold hardiness, shorten the time between planting and fruit production, and add resistance to pests. The scion is grafted onto the rootstock, and the two pieces of plant grow together to form one plant.

The swelling on a tree trunk indicates the graft union where the rootstock (bottom) and scion (top) of a fruit plant grow together.

In the Mid-Atlantic rootstocks are equally valuable for their ability to add cold hardiness or disease resistance as they are for their ability to control size (which is discussed in the "Growing Tree Fruits and Nuts in the Mid-Atlantic" section on page 86).

## Bloom Time and Pollination Requirements

Fruit plants have to be able to flower in order to produce fruits. Most fruit plant flowers need to be pollinated, and some need to be cross-pollinated with pollen from another tree.

When selecting fruit trees and shrubs for your home orchard, pay attention to whether a plant is self-fertile or self-pollinating (in which case you can plant just one plant and still get fruit), or if the plant requires cross-

A fruit tree orchard shows trees in various stages of blooming.

pollination (in which case, you need at least two plants). If you have limited space, go for self-fertile plants.

For trees requiring cross-pollination, bloom time also matters. If one tree or shrub is finished blooming before the one you bought to cross-pollinate it, neither will bear fruit. Apples, peaches, pears, and other flowering fruits are categorized into groups based on blooming times. You need to plant at least two from each group in order to get good pollination and fruit set.

Pay attention to pollination requirements when purchasing fruit plants. Otherwise, you could find yourself with healthy plants that never produce a harvest.

### Pest and Disease Resistance

Fruit trees and shrubs are susceptible to an alarming number of pest and disease problems. There are sprays and treatments that you can use to get rid of the problems, but you can give yourself a head start by choosing resistant plants. In grafted fruit plants, both the scion and the rootstock play a part in disease resistance. Pay attention to the recommendations in individual plant profiles.

### Chilling Hours Required

Fruit trees require a certain number of "chilling hours," or hours when the air temperature is below 45°F. Most fruit trees have chilling hour requirements that correspond to the length of time a plant will remain dormant before flowering. Chilling hours are required in many plants to trigger a break in dormancy, leading to blooming.

Temperatures above 60°F reverse chilling hours accumulated. If you plant a tree that requires 500 chilling hours in an area that receives only 300 hours, the plant will not flower and will not produce fruit.

Chilling hours are discussed in more detail in individual plant profiles. Recommended plant varieties for each area of the Mid-Atlantic have been selected, in part, with chilling hours in mind.

### End Use

Fruit trees and plants need a lot more care, for a much longer time, than other edibles. When picking out what you're going to plant, think about what you like to eat. Many gardeners find themselves branching out and trying new things if those new things come from their own gardens, but you want to be realistic. How many figs can you eat? There's no reason to plant six plants unless you're going into business making fig jam for everyone in your city. You don't need twelve apple trees if you're not going to put up quarts and quarts of apple butter.

Only plant things you like to eat, and only plant trees that will bear a manageable harvest for you.

## Planning a Fruit Garden

How many of each fruit do you plant? How much room do you need? The number of plants depends on the size of the plant, the yield you hope to harvest, and whether the plants require cross-pollination.

You can start small with two apple trees, four to six blackberry plants, four to six blueberry plants, and twelve strawberries.

---

### GROWING TIP

If you have more fruit than you know what to do with, check with local food pantries, homeless shelters, and meal programs. Some cities have "gleaning" programs, where volunteers will come and pick your extra harvest and take it to a needy charity prepared to make use of it. Other food banks can accept and distribute your fresh produce. Don't let fresh food go to waste, if you can help it.

Apples ready for harvest

Or you can tuck a few fruit trees along your lot line, add a row of blackberries near the vegetable garden, and devote a couple of rows or a raised bed from the vegetable garden to strawberries.

For me, the more fruit I can grow, the better. I have *never* had a problem giving away extra homegrown anything. The mistake most fruit gardeners make is not planting enough of each type of plant, thus limiting (or downright preventing) good pollination and fruit set.

My only exception to this rule is figs, which are prolific producers. Nobody needs more than one fig plant. They're like rabbits, only they're plants.

## Caring for Fruits

Each type of fruit plant has its own specific schedule of care, but there are maintenance tasks that are important to all fruit plants. You will need to make time to take care of these tasks in your fruit garden.

Parts of a Fruit Tree

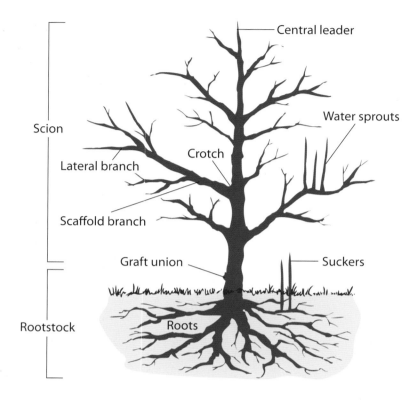

To understand the directions in the plant profiles, you need to be able to identify the parts of a fruit tree.

**Rootstock:** The bottom of the tree; the roots.

**Scion:** The top of the tree; the portion that produces fruit.

**Graft union:** The place on the tree where the rootstock meets the scion.

**Central leader:** The main trunk of the tree. (Apples and pears are pruned with a central leader. Peaches and plums are not.)

**Water sprout:** A branch that grows straight up from a scaffold branch on the fruit tree. Water sprouts do not produce fruit and should be removed.

**Scaffold branch:** A main horizontal branch from which fruiting spurs or branches grow.

**Lateral branch:** A smaller branch growing off of a scaffold branch. Lateral branches grow out, not up, and produce fruiting stems called spurs.

**Crotch:** The angle of a scaffold branch to the tree. Wider crotch angles are more stable and produce less breakage than narrow angles.

**Suckers:** Sprouts coming up from the rootstock. Sometimes suckers come from the stem below the graft union, and sometimes they appear to sprout right out of the soil. They should always be pruned off. Never put systemic weedkiller on a sucker. You can kill the whole tree.

## Pruning

Pruning isn't just for fruit trees. Grapes, blackberry bushes, and blueberries also require pruning. You'll prune to control the size of the plants, to get rid of old growth and encourage new growth, to increase sunlight penetration into the tree canopy, and to allow for airflow. Pruning helps establish the architecture of fruit trees and the renewal of blackberry patches.

Most pruning is done in winter when plants are dormant. A few plants benefit from summer pruning. This is noted in the individual plant profiles.

### PRUNING TOOLS

Here are the tools that you need in order to prune:

**Hand pruners**

**A** Hand pruners have a cutting blade and an anchor blade. They're good for pruning, deadheading, and cutting bamboo stakes.

**Pruning saw**

**B** Pruning saws fold up for easy toting in the garden basket. They are handy for cutting branches over 2 inches in diameter.

**Loppers**

**C** Loppers are like big hand pruners. They have the same type of cutting blade, but usually it is larger. Loppers also have longer handles. They're good for trimming shrubs and tree branches that are out of arm's reach.

**D**

**Pole pruning saw**

**D** If you grow semidwarf or standard-sized fruit trees, a pole pruner with both a lopping and a saw attachment is a handy tool. You'll use the saw just like you'd use a pruning saw, only with a longer handle. The lopping attachment will have a string to pull to engage the cutting blade. With a pole pruner, you can reach higher up into the tree without having to climb a ladder.

## PRUNING TECHNIQUES

Once the plants are in the ground, the most crucial aspect of fruit tree care is pruning. Individual instructions for fruit tree pruning are listed in the plant profiles. Here are the basics.

### Why Prune?

- To encourage new growth
- To let light and air into the tree
- To establish good structure (which makes it easier to harvest fruits)
- To control size

Fruit trees are usually pruned into scaffolds (apples, pears) or in an open-vase shape (peaches, plums). The scaffold method establishes a central leader with branches that decrease in length as you move up the tree. The open-vase shape establishes several main lateral branches that bear fruit. You can use heading cuts, thinning cuts, and renewal pruning to establish these shapes.

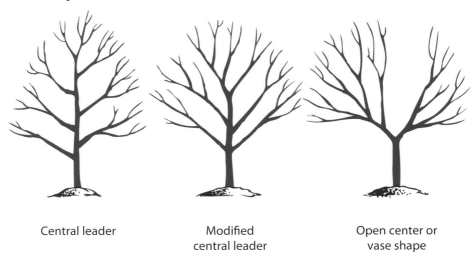

Central leader     Modified central leader     Open center or vase shape

Fruit trees are shaped by pruning. Apples should be pruned in a pyramid-like shape, while peaches and plums are pruned in an open, vase shape.

## TYPES OF PRUNING

**Heading cuts:** When you cut off the end of a branch, that's called a heading cut. The response of the plant will be to produce more side-shoots below where you made the heading cut.

**Thinning cuts:** When you remove some of the "bulk" or interior branches by cutting them all the way back to the main stem, you're making thinning cuts.

Heading cuts involve cutting off the ends of plant branches.

Thinning cuts involve removing some of the interior growth of the plant.

Renewal pruning is the process of removing one-third of the plant's growth each year.

**Renewal pruning:** This is a process most often used with shrubs, but which can also be applied to fruit trees, whereby you remove at least one-third of the old growth on the plant each year, stimulating new growth.

Pruning stimulates fresh new growth that will produce fruit. Old orchards are brought back to life by careful pruning of the old trees. Remember: When you prune fruit trees, it's like cutting hair—the plants will grow back.

**Thinning:** Fruit trees require thinning in order to produce larger fruits. The trees will self-thin about halfway through summer. You'll know this has happened, because suddenly a bunch of little fruits will be lying all over the ground. You can go through after this and continue to selectively thin. Pick fruits so that there is only one fruit every 4 to 6 inches along a branch.

## How to Remove Large Branches

When you need to remove a large branch (anything that requires a pruning saw), use the following three-cut pruning technique.

**1** Make the first cut on the underside of the branch, about 6 inches from the tree trunk. You'll only cut one-fourth to one-third of the way through the branch.

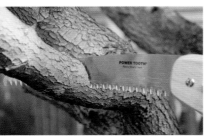

**2** Make the second cut farther out on the branch from the first cut. Cut the branch all the way off. The branch will probably break off while you're cutting it. That is why you made the first cut on the underside of the tree—to help the branch break in the direction you want without stripping the bark off the branch.

**3** You can see the finished second cut, here. At the very bottom of the cut edge, you can see where part of the branch ripped. Do not make a cut that strips the bark off of a tree branch.

**4** Cut off the branch stub remaining on the tree. Place the pruning saw just outside of the branch collar, which is the bark swelling between the branch and the main trunk. Saw through to remove the stub. Do not cut the branch flush with the tree trunk, or you'll hurt the tree's chances of healing itself.

**5** In this picture, you can see that there's still about ¼ to ½ inch of branch left to allow the branch collar to heal. Never cover pruning cuts with tar, concrete, or sealant. The tree will heal itself if left alone. Sealant or tar creates a dark, moist environment that is perfect for bacteria to grow in. Sealing a cut can actually hurt the tree. If you follow this pruning technique, it will heal itself.

## Staking and Support

Most landscape trees do not need to be staked when first planted, but many fruit trees do. Blackberries and raspberries require some sort of trellis to climb up for support. Fruits can be shallow rooted, which makes them easily dislodged by wind. Plan to stake newly planted trees and to construct sturdy trellising systems for newly planted vining fruits.

Other care considerations unique to different types of fruit plants are discussed in more detail in the individual plant profiles.

## Pest Control and Harvest Protection

Fruit pest control depends upon the pest and the host plant. Some pests are controlled with a spray of horticultural oil when the plants are not leafed out. Other pests have to be controlled while fruit is developing on the trees.

Pest control on fruits never stops, because observation of the trees and plants never stops. Different pests are active at different times of the year. Make it a habit to cruise your fruit tree orchard and look at the plants. If something seems amiss, take a cutting or take some pictures and identify the problem. If you're having trouble, consult your county extension service.

If birds are a problem, use netting to keep them from carrying away your harvest before you can.

---

**GROWING TIP**

Extremely cold temperatures can freeze flower buds. Some plants can tolerate more cold than their flower buds can, which means the trees might live through a cold snap, but the flowers won't. No flowers equals no fruit.

Temperature fluctuations also cause problems—mostly for plants that need to be cross-pollinated with pollen from another plant. Some areas of the Mid-Atlantic are notorious for temperature fluctuations. It can be 60°F one day and 10°F two nights later. These temperature fluctuations can cause plants to break dormancy and flower early. If you have three apple trees and one tree flowers early while the other two trees flower normally, the early-flowering plant can miss being pollinated. If all three plants pollinate during a freakishly warm stretch of early February when none of the insects that pollinate them are active, they will miss being pollinated.

Dwarf pear trees are easily managed from ground-level, as they grow no taller than 10 feet or so.

## Growing Tree Fruits and Nuts in the Mid-Atlantic

Growing fruit trees is as rewarding as it can be frustrating. To get good fruit tree growth and robust harvests requires patience (it can take a while for plants to bear fruit) and vigilance (there are always insects and diseases waiting in the wings to destroy your harvest).

As has been discussed frequently in this book, choosing local sources for your plants is an important part of success in fruit tree growing. Another factor in selecting a tree is deciding upon the size that you want.

You can purchase standard (or seedling) trees grown on their own rootstocks. These fruit trees can grow from 20 to 30 feet tall. Most home gardeners look for semidwarf and dwarf fruit trees. Semidwarf trees (10 to 20 feet at maturity) are best, if you have the space. They are usually longer lived, establish deeper roots, and have more disease resistance than dwarf trees (5 to 10 feet at maturity).

Aside from the natural height of the tree (apples are naturally taller than peaches), the rootstock usually determines the size of the tree.

## Find Your Favorite Fruits and Nuts

You can check the index at the back of the book, but you can also use the alphabetical list below to find your favorite edibles.

Standard pear trees grow much larger.

## PLANTING NEW FRUIT TREES

When planting new dwarf or semi-dwarf fruit trees, it helps if you can stake the trees. These trees are grafted onto rootstocks and can be more fragile than non-grafted "seedling" standard-sized trees. Staking the trees will keep them from blowing over in the wind as they're establishing their root systems. It helps to stake these trees for up to two or three years (re-setting the wires yearly to allow the tree to grow without wires cutting into the bark). What happens if you don't stake? They will blow over. I speak from experience. All of my nectarine trees are now growing at an angle because I was too lazy to stake them or to pull them up after a hurricane! But, it doesn't take a hurricane to knock them over. If you want healthy trees, start them right by staking.

# APPLE *(Malus domestica)*

With the right selection of variety, apples can be grown in the Mid-Atlantic.

You'll never want to eat a store-bought apple again after you taste one that you harvested from your own tree. They're sweeter, crunchier, juicier, and have so much more flavor! Your own apples also won't have the waxy coating that commercial growers put on their fruits to keep them "fresh" during transit.

All apples that we grow today are actually two-part plants. The top of the plant, which produces the fruit we eat, is called the scion. Rather than growing from seed, scions are cuttings from other plants of the same species. The bottom of the plant is called the rootstock. Rootstocks can cause a scion to grow more slowly, increase cold hardiness, shorten the time between planting and fruit production, and add resistance to pests.

When you purchase an apple tree, you select not only the scion (or top), but often a particular rootstock as well. Nursery catalogs sometimes offer different choices—allowing you to purchase, say, a Gala apple with a dwarfing or semidwarfing rootstock. A "standard" tree is one that grows to full size without the benefit of a dwarfing rootstock. The size that you select depends on how much space you have to grow the tree, the type of soil in which you will be planting it, and the average low temperature for your area.

## ■ *Recommended Varieties*

When selecting apple trees, you need to think about two things:

- ■ The preferred size (and thus the preferred rootstock)
- ■ Bloom time for pollination

### Rootstocks Suitable for the Mid-Atlantic

Semidwarf rootstocks will produce trees that are about two-thirds the size of a standard tree. Common semidwarf rootstocks for the Mid-Atlantic include MM.106, MM.111, and M.7. These rootstocks cut the time from planting to fruit production from ten years down to four to six years.

Dwarf rootstocks produce trees that are half to one-third the size of a standard tree and reduce time from planting to fruiting from ten years to two to four years. Common dwarf rootstocks for the Mid-Atlantic include M.9 and M.26.

### Planting Trees for Cross-Pollinating

In order to get apples, you need to plant at least two trees that bloom at the same time so that they can cross-pollinate each other. Some trees are sterile and do not produce fertile pollen. If you plant one of those trees, you need to plant at least two others in order to get apples on all of the trees.

This chart shows apple varieties suited for our area, and trees that work well as pollinators. Trees marked with an asterisk (*) have sterile pollen.

### Apple Tree Varieties and Cross-Pollinator

Variety characteristics in order of ripening

| Variety | Fruit Color | Fruit Use | Relative Bloom Time | Potential Cross Pollinators |
|---|---|---|---|---|
| Gala | Yellow-orange to red | Fresh | Early to midseason | Golden Delicious |
| Empire | Dark red over green background | Fresh, cooking | Early | Golden or Red Delicious, Gala |
| Jonagold* | Yellow with light red stripes | Fresh, cooking | Midseason | Gala, Empire |
| Golden Delicious | Yellow-green to light yellow | Fresh, cooking | Midseason to late | Red Delicious, Gala |
| Red Delicious | Red | Fresh | Early | Golden Delicious, Gala |
| Stayman* | Blush to red | Fresh, cooking | Midseason | Gala, Golden or Red Delicious |
| Rome | Blush to red | Fresh, cooking | Late | Fuji, Braeburn |
| Braeburn | Green with light red blush | Fresh | Midseason | Rome, Fuji |
| Fuji | Green with red stripes | Fresh | Midseason | Rome, Braeburn |
| Anna | Red blush | Fresh | Early | Dorsett Golden |
| Dorsett Golden | Yellow | Fresh | Early | Anna |
| Arkansas Black | Dark red | Fresh, cider | Midseason | Braeburn |

*Tree has sterile pollen.

Varieties for Different Areas of the Mid-Atlantic
Plant these apple trees in your Mid-Atlantic garden for a bumper crop in the fall.

Lodi, Earlycrisp, Redfree, Gala, Jonagold, Red Delicious, Golden Delicious, Empire, Rome, Winesap, York, Fuji, Arkansas Black, Granny Smith, Honeycrisp.

## Planting

Apples are tree fruits and are planted the same way you would plant any tree. Refer to the instructions on page 47. You can plant apple trees at any point during the year, although it is best to avoid planting them during the worst heat of summer (mid-June through August).

Also important in terms of planting is spacing. Apples need to be planted close enough to each other for pollination. Plant standard trees no more than 75 feet apart, semidwarf trees no more than 45 feet apart, and dwarf trees no more than 25 feet apart.

When planting grafted apple trees, make sure that the graft union (where the scion meets the rootstock) is at least 5 inches above the soil. Stake grafted trees for the first two to three years to ensure that they take root and, literally, stay together while getting established in the garden.

## Maintenance

Once planted and staked, the primary maintenance concern is pruning. You need to water the trees as they are becoming established and fertilize yearly in spring by spreading a balanced 10-10-10 fertilizer according to package instructions around the root zone of the tree.

To allow trees to establish themselves well, remove all fruit that forms during the first three years when it first starts appearing—before it ripens. (Difficult, I know, but your trees will be healthier in the long run.)

Pruning is the critical type of maintenance for apple trees, though. From the moment you plant a tree, the way you prune it and train it will determine whether it is healthy and has good structure for bearing fruits or whether it is susceptible to breakage in high winds, breakage from heavy fruit loads, or low fruit production from lack of light.

When pruning fruit trees, the goal is to establish good architecture. This allows air circulation in the canopy (top of the tree), permits light penetration (sunlight must reach the inner branches for fruit production), and creates a branch structure that can withstand wind and the weight of fruit on a branch.

## Pruning to Maintain Established Trees

Once the tree has become established (four or more years), you'll need to prune to maintain good architecture and encourage fruiting. Always remove water sprouts, which are branches that grow straight up from side branches. These aren't growing in the right direction to produce good long-term shape and they won't bear fruit.

## Pruning to Establish New Trees

This diagram shows how to prune a tree purchased from a nursery:

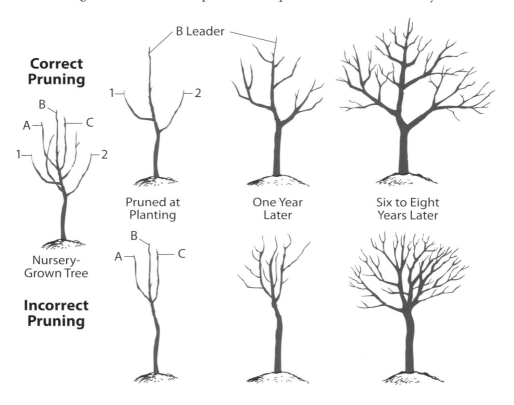

**Correct Pruning**

Nursery-Grown Tree

Pruned at Planting

One Year Later

Six to Eight Years Later

**Incorrect Pruning**

In addition to structural maintenance, you'll prune to encourage fruiting. Some apple trees produce fruits from spurs, which are small, compressed, nubby stems along the branches. It's a rule of thumb that the fewer fruits there are on the tree, the bigger the fruits will be. If there are too many spurs on the tree, you can use hand pruners to simply snip off the spurs at even intervals. If the tree

Apple tree spur

doesn't have enough spurs, you can cut off the end of the branch, which will cause the plants to sprout more spurs along the branches. Some apples bear fruit from the tips of branches. Prune these trees by cutting back the ends of branches by 8 to 10 inches, leaving five or six buds on the branches.

The overall guiding principle of pruning all fruit trees is to maintain a somewhat triangular shape. This allows light to reach every part of the tree. (Remember that no light equals no fruit.)

## ■ Pest Problems

Apples are members of the rose family (along with many other edible fruit plants) and are susceptible to a wide variety of pests and diseases. Plant selection is key in growing healthy apple plants, as is identifying plants in your garden that could be harboring pests and diseases. Crabapples, junipers, and arborvitae all harbor the cedar-apple rust pest. If you want to grow apples in your garden, you might consider getting rid of these three ornamentals.

Cedar apple rust

Other apple problems include apple scab, powdery mildew, and fireblight. Try to plant cultivars that are resistant to these diseases. Spraying dormant oil during winter can control many diseases. Apple maggots are the worst insect pests. To control them, hang sticky traps—available in garden centers and home-improvement stores—in the trees. You can also protect individual fruits by placing a plastic bag around each fruit and attaching it with a clothespin.

If you have trouble identifying what pest, disease, or cultural problem (caused by

Apple scab

maintenance or lack thereof rather than an insect or disease) is plaguing your apple tree, take pictures, including close-ups, and cut a branch and take it to your county extension service.

## ■ *Harvesting*

Apples are ready for harvest when they easily come off the tree in your hand. Don't rip apples from the tree, as you can damage the spurs or buds that will produce fruit next year.

### Days from Bloom to Harvest for Commonly Grown Apple Types

| Variety | Days from bloom to harvest |
|---|---|
| Lodi | 65 |
| Ginger Gold | 100 |
| Gala | 105 |
| McIntosh | 130 |
| Red Delicious | 150 |
| Golden Delicious | 155 |
| Rome | 160 |
| Stayman | 165 |
| Winesap | 170 |
| York | 170 |
| Fuji | 180 |
| Granny Smith | 195 |

**GROWING TIP**

Apple trees will self-thin in the middle of the summer. Do not be alarmed when you see some of the fruits drop off the tree. It's a natural process that will result in larger fruits ripening in fall.

Pick up dropped fruits, and rake and remove leaves each year.

Certain apple diseases will overwinter in dead leaves and fruits.

Control pests by practicing good garden hygiene.

# CHERRY *(Prunus avium, Prunus cerasus)*

Who doesn't love cherry pie? And don't you love summer, when you can finally add a Tupperware full of sweet cherries to your lunch box? Not all gardeners in the Mid-Atlantic can grow cherries, but the ones who can are lucky and should definitely plant a few trees. Plan on growing cherries if you live in zones 6 and 7 in the Mid-Atlantic. (Gardeners in the Coastal Plain area and Piedmont could have issues with heat in the summer.)

## ■ *Recommended Varieties*

There are tart cherries and sweet cherries. Some sweet cherries are self-fertile and do not require a pollinator trees, others do require cross-pollination, so make sure to pick out compatible varieties (bloom at the same time) when shopping. Most tart cherries are self-pollinating.

**Sweet cherry varieties:** 'Vista', 'Ulster', 'Viva', 'Hartland', 'Royalton', 'Emperor Francis'.
**Tart cherry varieties:** 'Jubileum', 'Dantube', 'Montmorency', 'Surefire', 'Balaton', 'Northstar'.

Tart cherries grow better than sweet cherries in the humid climate of the Mid-Atlantic.

## ■ *Planting*

Cherries grow best in full sun and well-drained soil. Plant the trees, taking care to ensure that the graft union between the rootstock and scion (top and bottom) is at least 3 inches above the soil.

Follow instructions for planting trees on page 47. Stake the trees for the first two years after planting.

## ■ *Maintenance*

Cherry trees are highly susceptible to drought. Water the trees daily after planting and do not let them dry out. Mulch around newly-planted trees to keep moisture in around the root zone.

Tart cherry pruning is similar to peach tree pruning, in terms of shape. You'll prune tart cherries to an open vase shape or semi-open vase shape. Prune sweet cherries as you'd prune an apple. Cherries fruit on spurs, like apples, so treat individual branches as you would apple trees, being careful not to knock off or break off the spurs.

Prune cherry trees in mid-summer. Do not prune during cool, wet spring weather.

## ■ *Pest Problems*

There are some diseases that affect cherry trees, but they usually do not cause problems for the home gardener. Just take care to rake away all leaf and fruit debris at the end of the season so that disease spores can't overwinter right under the tree.

Birds are one of the most annoying pests of cherry trees. You can cover smaller trees with bird netting, but if you have a larger tree, hang a "scary eye" balloon in the tree (a yellow beach ball with red circles with black centers) to scare the birds away.

## ■ *Harvesting*

Cherries are ready to harvest when they easily fall off the tree. Sweet cherries will be firm, while tart cherries will be starting to soften.

# CHESTNUT *(Castanea* hybrids*)*

The American chestnut (*Castanea dentate)* used to comprise 25 percent of trees in eastern hardwood forests. Chestnut blight took out most of these trees. To grow chestnuts today, you need to look for a Chinese-American hybrid tree. You can also grow a straight Chinese chestnut (*C. mollissima)*. Once established, these nut trees are easy to grow.

Be sure to plant your chestnut tree where the spiny husks that fall to the ground won't be a problem.

## ◼ Recommended Varieties

Plant what you can find. Chestnuts can be difficult to track down. You might have to order online. Chestnuts do require cross-pollination, so make sure to plant a pollinator tree. Some nurseries sell "chestnut seedling pollinators" just for this purpose.

## ◼ Planting

Chestnut trees are large, so plant them where they have room to grow to heights of 40 to 50 feet. Be careful to avoid planting under power lines. Plant chestnut trees 30 to 40 feet apart.

## ◼ Maintenance

Mulch trees with compost and water frequently (at least 10 to 15 gallons per week) when trees are first establishing themselves. Test the soil where chestnut trees are growing to ensure proper levels of zinc. Zinc deficiency can cause bronzing and mottling of leaves; early defoliation; dead twigs in tops of trees; abnormally small nuts; small yellowish, chlorotic leaves; and short, thin twigs growing on older scaffold branches with rosettes of small, yellowish green leaves at the tips.

## ■ *Pest Problems*

Squirrels are one of the worst pests affecting all nut trees. This is primarily because they eat your harvest before you can. To protect trees from squirrels, wrap the trunk with a metal shield, 5 feet off the ground. You can attach the shield with spikes that you withdraw slightly each year as the tree grows.

Chestnut trees can grow to be 40 to 50 feet tall.

## ■ *Harvesting*

Start harvesting nuts when they start to fall. Lay a clean sheet under the trees and shake the branches to loosen the nuts. Once you harvest them from the tree, lay them in a single layer in a warm, dry place to dry out. You can freeze nuts in resealable plastic bags until you're ready to use them.

# PEACH & NECTARINE
## *(Prunus persica)*

Homegrown peaches and nectarines are so delicious, sweet, and juicy because they can be left on the tree until they are ripe, instead of being picked hard and unripe to withstand shipping. However, both peaches and nectarines are more difficult to grow than most other fruit trees. They are pickier about pruning and pest control and are susceptible to a huge variety of pests, diseases, and cultural problems such as pruning at the wrong time or under or over watering. Eating a peach that you harvest yourself is worth the effort, though. Just be prepared, if you plant peaches and nectarines, to put in some extra work to get the reward.

## ■ *Recommended Varieties*

California-grown peaches are not suitable for Mid-Atlantic gardens. When selecting your plants, it is imperative that you purchase locally grown trees of varieties that have been specifically bred to grow well in the Mid-Atlantic.

Peach

### *Rootstocks*
Rootstock selection is as important as scion selection. 'Lovell' and 'Halford' are two high-performing rootstocks for the Mid-Atlantic.

### *Varieties*
**Peaches:** 'Belle of Georgia', 'Contender' (the most cold hardy), 'Early Red Haven', 'Elberta', 'Loring', 'Madison', 'Redhaven', 'Reliance'

**Nectarines:** 'Hardired', 'Flavortop', 'Red Gold'

Whenever possible, consult with your county extension service for recommendations on varieties and suppliers. You can buy a peach or nectarine tree anywhere and enjoy the flowers, but you can't buy one anywhere and expect to get fruits.

## ■ *Planting*

Plant peaches in late fall through early spring. Peaches and nectarines are self-fertile, so spacing is not as critical when planting these trees. Location is important. Peaches are susceptible to cold snaps. Plant these trees near the top of a hill or slope so that cold air can drain down and away from the trees.

Peaches and nectarines need well-drained soil to establish healthy root systems. They are not at all tolerant of heavy, poorly drained soils.

Follow instructions for planting trees on page 47 and stake peaches and nectarines for the first two years after planting.

Nectarine

## Maintenance

Peaches are fast growers that do not need extra fertilizer. The biggest aspects of peach maintenance are pruning, thinning, and pest control. Prune peach trees to maintain an upright vase shape. Peaches produce lots of side branches, about half of which need to be removed yearly in order to channel energy into production of fewer, larger fruits. Peaches will self-thin in summer, dropping as many as half of the fruits. You can further thin peaches, leaving one peach or nectarine to mature every 5 or 6 inches along the branch.

To keep peaches productive (they produce fruit on one-year-old branches), prune after the plants have finished fruiting and you have finished harvesting. Remove one-third of the branches each year to keep new, fresh wood growing.

## Pest Problems

Give yourself a leg up on pest control by planting resistant varieties. Even this won't spare your plants from all pests. If you want to grow fresh peaches and nectarines, you will have to follow a pest-control program. Whether you use organic or synthetic pesticides is up to you, but you won't have peaches without being vigilant about pests.

Diseases are a bigger problem than insects with peaches and nectarines. Peach leaf curl, brown rot, powdery mildew, peach scab, bacterial spot, and other diseases are problems with peaches. The main insect pest is *plum curculio*. Use fungicides and dormant oil in spring before the plants bloom in order to control diseases. Use a properly labeled insecticide to treat plum curculio right after blossom drop to treat this insect.

## Harvesting

Peaches are ready for harvest starting in early summer and continuing through late summer, depending on the variety. The fruits should easily come off the tree without yanking, and they should be slightly soft to the touch.

# PEAR *(Pyrus* spp.*)*

Mid-Atlantic gardeners can grow both European and Asian varieties of pears. Asian pears have rounder, firmer fruits than the European varieties. Both types are prolific producers—a couple of trees is enough for the home gardener. It can take up to nine years for pear trees to bear fruit, though varieties grown on dwarf rootstocks will bear fruits earlier. Asian pears will often bear two to three years after planting—another reason to try these unusual fruits.

Espaliered pear tree

## Recommended Varieties

**European:** 'Harrow Delight', 'Stark Honeysweet', 'Moonglow', 'Harvest Queen', 'Potomac', Buerre D'Anjou', 'Harrow Sweet', 'Bosc'.
**Asian:** 'Shinseiki', 'Hosui', 'Kosui', 'Shinseiki', 'Olympic'.

## Planting

Plant pears in full sun in well-drained, nutrient-rich soil in late fall through early spring. Add compost to the planting hole and use compost as a mulch around the plants. Plant two or more trees, 10 to 15 feet apart, so that they can cross-pollinate each other. While most Asian pears are self-fertile, they'll produce a bigger harvest if they have a cross-pollinating tree nearby.

## Maintenance

Pears, once established, do not need extra water. They never need extra fertilizer. As with other fruit trees, pruning is the most important aspect of maintenance (beyond pest control).

Prune pears in late winter in a similar manner to apple trees—to encourage airflow and light penetration. Maintain a triangular shape with a strong central leader (single central trunk) and scaffold (layers of branches that progressively get shorter toward the top of the tree).

Pears bear fruit on three- to ten-year-old spurs. Do not prune to remove spurs, as making more pruning cuts will open more areas for diseases to attack the plants. You will want to renewal prune by removing 10 percent of the canopy each year to promote new growth.

To encourage production of fewer, larger fruits, thin fruits when they're 1 inch in diameter, leaving one fruit every 6 inches along each branch.

## ■ Pest Problems

Fireblight is a big enough problem with pears that it is important to plant resistant varieties. You'll know that your tree has a fireblight problem if the leaves on specific branches turn brown and dry up, seemingly overnight. It's difficult to control this disease. You can control insect problems that affect pears, such as the aphid-like pear psylla, by spraying trees with dormant oil during winter.

## ■ Harvesting

Pears will be ready to harvest 100 to 140 days after flowering, depending on the variety. Allow Asian pears to ripen fully on the tree and then pick them. Asian pears will keep up to three months in the refrigerator. Harvest European pears when they are still firm to the touch and allow them to soften indoors.

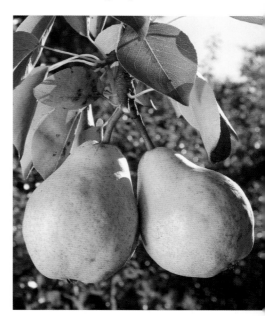

It can take several years for a pear tree to bear fruit.

## GROWING TIPS

Pear trees can have narrow branch angles that make the branches susceptible to breaking from high winds. You can train the branches to have a wider angle by hanging weights on the individual branches when they are young. That sounds weird, but it works.

If you have space along a wall, you can espalier a pear tree to grow flat against a trellis.

# PECAN *(Carya illinoinensis)*

Pecans are in the hickory nut family and thus have a fond place in my memory. One of the houses I lived in as a child came with a fairly mature yard and garden. There were two big hickory trees in the front yard. I always looked forward to playing "cook in the kitchen," making mud pies with the nuts. Occasionally I tried to crack them and eat them, too—quite a task for a seven-year-old. To have success growing pecans in the Mid-Atlantic, make sure to plant varieties that are resistant to diseases found here. You also need to plant at least two trees of different cultivars to get the best nut harvest.

## ■ *Recommended Varieties*

Pecans require cross-pollination from another variety of tree. The number of varieties and the relationships between them is too complex for this book. It's worth reviewing pecan selection information with your cooperative extension before purchasing. Here are a few suggestions, though.

'Pawnee' and 'Posey' are hardy and will pollinate each other. 'Major' pollinates 'Colby' and 'Stark Surecrop'.

Container-grown trees are easier to establish than bare-root trees and can be planted at any time. Do not purchase a container-grown tree that is larger than 5 or 6 feet tall. Pecans establish taproots as they grow, which makes them hard to transplant. Bare-root trees should be planted outside from late fall to early winter.

## ■ *Planting*

Pecan trees are large, so plant them where they have room to grow to heights of 40 to 50 feet. Be careful to avoid planting under power lines. Plant pecan trees 60 to 80 feet apart.

Pecan trees are large, full-sized landscape trees.

## ■ *Maintenance*

Mulch trees with compost, and water frequently (at least 10 to 15 gallons per week) when trees are first establishing themselves. Test the soil where pecan trees are growing to ensure proper levels of zinc. Zinc deficiency can cause bronzing and mottling of leaves; early defoliation; dead twigs in tops of trees; abnormally small nuts; small yellowish, chlorotic leaves; and short, thin twigs growing on older scaffold branches, with rosettes of small, yellowish green leaves at the tips.

## ■ *Pest Problems*

Squirrels are one of the worst pests affecting pecan trees. This is primarily because they eat your harvest before you can. To protect trees from squirrels, wrap the trunk with a metal shield, 5 feet off the ground. You can attach the shield with spikes that you withdraw slightly each year as the tree grows.

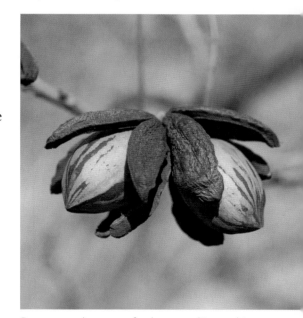

Pecan scab is a major disease problem for pecans. You can mostly control the spread of this disease by cleaning up leaves, twigs, and nuts from the previous year and throwing them away (not composting).

Pecans can be eaten fresh or used in cooking and baking.

## ■ *Harvesting*

Start harvesting nuts when they start to fall. Lay a clean sheet under the trees and shake the branches to loosen the nuts. Once you harvest them from the tree, lay them in a single layer in a warm, dry place to dry out. You can freeze nuts in resealable plastic bags until you're ready to use them.

'Great Wall' persimmon is an Asian type.

# PERSIMMON *(Diospyros virginiana* [American], *Diospyros kaki* [Asian]*)*

There are two types of persimmons: American and Asian (or Oriental). A huge native American persimmon tree grew over the sidewalk next to the tiny house where I lived in college, across from the Horticulture Building, at Purdue University. I wish I had taken advantage of the fruits by cooking them instead of cursing the mess they made when we tracked them into the house. American persimmons have to be picked when ripe for best flavor. Asian persimmons can be picked when slightly underripe.

## ■ *Recommended Varieties*

American persimmons require a male and female tree planted near each other in order to produce fruit. Asian persimmons are self-pollinating. They will only produce fruit in zones 7 or higher, though, which means not all gardeners in the Mid-Atlantic can grow them.

---

**GROWING TIP**

It's a myth that persimmons have to withstand a frost before they can be harvested. In fact, frost will damage fruits.

Persimmons can be difficult to locate, so you might just plant what you can find. A native American variety that grows well in the Mid-Atlantic is 'Prok'. 'Yates' is an extremely cold hardy variety.

'Saijo' is a good Oriental Persimmon for the Mid-Atlantic, hardy to zone 6. 'Tanenashi' is another choice, hardy to zone 7.

## Planting

Persimmons can be messy. Select a site where the tree will not grow over a driveway or walkway—unless you want to track the mess into your house. Plant cross-pollinating native varieties at least 50 feet apart so that the two trees don't crowd each other. Plant Asian varieties 15 to 20 feet apart.

## Maintenance

Persimmons are drought tolerant and low maintenance once established. Asian varieties are smaller and require pruning similar to apple tree pruning.

## Pest Problems

There are some pests that affect persimmon trees, but, by and large, it isn't feasible to control problems on a 40-foot tree. If the trees are grown in a diverse landscape, most problems will naturally resolve themselves.

## Harvesting

Pick fruits in fall when they're soft. Nonastringent Asian varieties can be harvested when they are still firm.

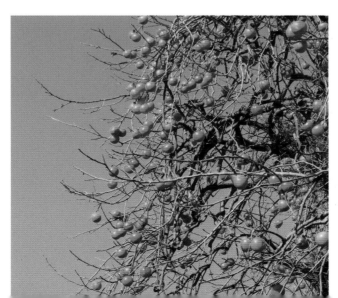

One persimmon tree will bear a lot of fruit.

# PLUM *(Prunus* spp.*)*

Buy a plum at the grocery store and it is likely to be hard and flavorless. Grow and harvest your own and you'll change your tune about eating these fruits. There are two main types of plums: European and Japanese. Dried plums, or prunes, are European plums. Japanese plums are juicy with thin skins. Excellent for fresh eating, these are the kinds most readily available in the grocery store. Asian plums grow best in warmer areas of the Mid-Atlantic, and European plums thrive in cooler regions of the Mid-Atlantic.

## ■ *Recommended Varieties*

Plums require a cross-pollinator tree of the same type. Japanese plums cross-pollinate other Japanese plums, and European plums cross-pollinate European plums. The 'Methley' variety of Japanese plums is self-fruitful and doesn't require another variety for pollination.

**Japanese:** 'Early Golden', 'Methley', 'Shiro'.
**European:** 'Earliblue', 'Blue Bell', 'Stanley', 'Shropshire'

Before settling on a variety, consult with your county extension service. Plums can be grafted onto rootstocks that are susceptible to nematodes. When shopping for plums, look for plants grafted onto 'Nemaguard', 'Guardian', 'Lovell', 'Halford', or 'Myrobalan' rootstocks.

## ■ *Planting*

Plant plums in full sun, 18 to 22 feet apart in soils with a pH of 6.0 to 6.5. Plums are tolerant of different soil types, growing equally well in heavier clay soils and sandy soils.

## ■ *Maintenance*

Plums benefit from being fertilized once a year in spring right after they finish blooming. Because they're heavy fruiters, these trees benefit from regular water during summer.

Prune plums in much the same way that you'd prune apples and pears—to let light into the trees, encourage air circulation, and create good branch scaffolding. Prune plums in late winter (after February 1).

When fruits are ½ inch in diameter, thin fruits to one every 4 to 5 inches along the branch.

## ■ *Pest Problems*

Plums are susceptible to brown rot, a fungal disease. Use fungicides labeled for use on peaches to treat this disease. Black knot is a disease that causes warty growths on branches. Cut off affected branches and throw away the

Fresh, home-grown plums make excellent eating.

pieces. (Do not compost diseased plant parts.) Plum curculio is one of the worst insect pests affecting plums. There are insecticides that will control this pest. Always follow instructions when using pesticides.

## ■ *Harvesting*

Plums are ready to harvest when the fruits have a white, waxy coating. Allow European plums to ripen fully before harvesting. Asian plums can be picked when they are slightly underripe. Be careful not to yank the fruits off the trees, because you don't want to break the fruiting spurs, which will bear again the following year.

---

**GROWING TIP**

The biggest difference in growing plums from growing other fruit trees is that you need to prune them to favor longer, outward-growing branches as opposed to a strictly triangular shape. This results in an open center, allowing plenty of light penetration.

Blackberries ripening for harvest

# FRUIT SHRUBS & BRAMBLES

If you're looking to get into fruit growing, starting with shrubs is a good plan. Fruit shrubs are forgiving, easy to care for, and are prolific producers once established. Blueberries, figs, and brambles (raspberries and blackberries) are the easiest to grow in the Mid-Atlantic. You might want to also experiment with growing less common fruits such as gooseberries. They make great pies!

## ■ *Landscaping with Fruit*

Edible landscaping is a hot topic. Rosalind Creasy is arguably the pioneer of planting your yard with edibles. The first edition of her book *Edible Landscaping* was published in 1982 and reissued as a second edition in 2010. If you want to see what you can really do with edibles by converting your entire yard to a fruit and vegetable garden, her book is amazing. Most people can't do that, though. But even if you're on the fence about turning your fence into a tomato trellis, you can at least tuck some Swiss chard or herbs into the perennial border.

It's easy to work fruit shrubs into the landscape. Blueberries are quite ornamental. They have beautiful fall color—their leaves turn bright red— a plus for any garden. Fig trees make excellent screening plants, because they have large leaves and lots of them. (They are deciduous, though, so they are less useful as a screen in winter.) A fence of blackberries is somehow friendlier than an actual fence. I have a blackberry fence between my house and my neighbor's, and I get more berries than we can eat from just six plants.

## ■ *Placing Fruit Shrubs in the Garden*

Fruit shrubs can be planted throughout the yard (provided that you plant at least two or three near each other if they need to be cross-pollinated) or along the edges of the property. Because fruit shrubs take up less space and throw less shade than fruit trees, you can also plant them in or around your vegetable garden. Plant taller varieties on the north side of the garden so that they don't shade other plants.

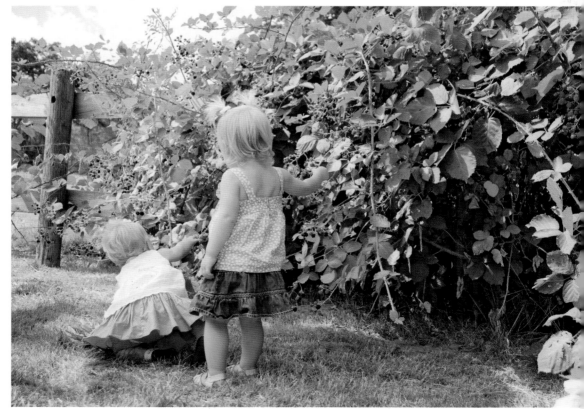

Get kids involved with gardening by letting them help harvest!

# BLUEBERRY *(Vaccinium* spp.*)*

Blueberries are one of the few widely grown fruits that are native to North America. Blueberries grow from Maine down to Georgia, over to Texas, and up to Wisconsin. Different varieties thrive in different locations. The key to success with blueberry growing is to choose the appropriate variety. Northern Highbush and Southern Highbush types are the best for Mid-Atlantic States.

## ■ *Recommended Varieties*

Cooler areas of the Mid-Atlantic should grow Northern Highbush blueberries. Warmer areas can grow Southern Highbush blueberries.

| Early Season | Mid Season | Late Season |
|---|---|---|
| Austin | Bluebelle | Baldwin |
| Brightwell | Briteblue | Centurion |
| Climax | Chaucer | Choice |
| Premier | Powderblue | Delite |
| Woodard | Tifblue | |

Northern Highbush blueberries grow well the Mountains and Plateau areas. Recommend cultivars include 'Darrow', 'Brigitta', 'Bluegold', 'Ozarkblue', 'Bluejay', and 'Patriot'. Southern Highbush blueberries grow well in the Piedmont and Coastal plain areas. Recommend cultivars include 'O'Neal', 'Reville', 'Cape Fear', 'Pamlico', 'Sampson', 'Duplin', 'Blueridge'.

Some blueberry varieties require a cross-pollinator, while others do not. Always check to see whether you need to plant two different cultivars when purchasing blueberry plants.

## ■ *Planting*

Plant blueberries in early spring through mid-summer. They grow well in acidic soil (the native soils of the eastern United States). If your soil is alkaline, you will have to add aluminum sulfate to lower the pH to below 6.0. (If you can get the pH to 4.5 to 5.5, that's even better.) Take this step at least three months before you plan to plant. Blueberries also need relatively high levels of organic matter in the soil. If you have sandy soil, amend the soil in the entire blueberry planting area by adding at least 4 inches of compost.

Blueberry plants provide fresh fruit in the summer and decorative foliage in cooler weather.

**GROWING TIP**

Establishment of acidic soil is critical with blueberries. Fail to prepare your soil, and you will not get the results you want.

If the leaves turn yellow with green veins, the pH of the soil is most likely off and needs to be checked. Iron deficiency can be a problem in high-pH soils. Add chelated iron to correct the problem.

## Maintenance

**Water:** Water every other day during the first six months after planting to encourage good establishment. After the first year, water twice a week during fruiting and once a week after plants have finished fruiting. Blueberries are shallow rooted, so they dry out quickly.

**Mulch:** Help keep the soil around blueberries moist by mulching with pine needles or shredded hardwood mulch.

**Fertilizer:** Do not fertilize during the first six months of growth. After the first six months, feed with a balanced fertilizer before the plants bloom and after you harvest the fruits, to encourage growth for next year. To maintain the acidity of the soil, you can also feed with fertilizer formulated for hollies.

**Pruning:** Prune blueberries in late winter or early spring. They do produce fruits on one-year-old growth, so don't hack the plant to the ground. If you do, you won't get any berries. You can prune a bit each year to keep the shrubs a manageable size. Renewal prune by selectively removing at least one-third of the oldest branches each year (throughout the shrub) to encourage new growth.

## Pest Problems

Birds are the most annoying pest problem with blueberries. You can throw nets over the shrubs once the fruits are reaching harvestable size in order to protect them. Blueberry maggots and cherry and cranberry fruitworms can be problems with blueberries. You'll see the webs they make. Cut off affected area and discard.

## Harvesting

Blueberry season runs from June through August. Pick berries as you plan to eat them for the freshest fruits. (They can stay on the shrubs for a while, so you don't have to pick the shrub clean all at once.) The easiest way to determine if the berries are ripe is to taste a few. You'll learn to recognize when they're ready to harvest.

For best eating, pick figs when they are soft to the touch.

# FIG *(Ficus carica)*

Figs are probably the most low-maintenance fruit plants you can grow. It took a trip to California for me to truly appreciate what you can do with figs in the kitchen. My new favorite fall sandwich is an open-faced, toasted sandwich made with goat cheese, caramelized onions, and figs and braised in the oven for a few minutes. When shopping for fig plants make sure to purchase figs that are cold-hardy. Figs can grow to be large and unruly, so stay on top of pruning to keep them inbounds.

## ■ *Recommended Varieties*

Only grow varieties of figs that do not require cross-pollination. Recommended varieties for cooler regions include 'Chicago Hardy' and 'Brown Turkey'.

## ■ *Planting*

Plant fig trees in late winter to early spring when they're dormant. Figs are fast growers and won't become well established if planted during summer. Plant figs in full sun to partial shade in nutrient-rich, well-drained soil. Give them room to grow, as they can reach up to 30 feet in height and spread.

## ■ *Maintenance*

**Water:** Give figs 1 inch of water per week during summer.

**Fertilizer:** Fertilize once a year with a balanced fertilizer just as the plants begin flowering.

**Pruning:** Figs need to be pruned mainly to keep them from taking over the landscape—they can get big. Prune figs in late winter while they are still dormant.

## ■ *Pest Problems*

Figs are fairly pest-free plants, making them ideal for home gardens. The biggest problem affecting figs is root knot nematodes. Buy certified nematode-free plants and inspect plants before planting them. If their roots look knobbly or knotty, do not plant them. Nematodes are hard to control once established in the landscape, so try to plant resistant varieties.

## ■ *Harvesting*

Figs taste best when harvested ripe. Pick figs when they are somewhat soft to the touch, and eat them within a few days.

---

**GROWING TIP**

Because figs can experience pruning via freezing temperatures (frost damage), grow figs as shrubs, not trees. That way, if the plant dies back, you'll still have some of it left to bear fruit next year.

# BLACKBERRY & RASPBERRY
## *(Rubus* spp.*)*

Blackberries and raspberries are "bramble" fruits. Brambles are part of the rose family. In fact, their flowers look a little bit like small wild roses. Blackberries and raspberries require similar care and have similar growth habits. Blackberries are easier to grow in the warmer parts of the Mid-Atlantic, though. A half-dozen blackberry or raspberry plants will give you a large harvest.

Blackberries are easy to grow throughout the Mid-Atlantic.

## ■ *Recommended Varieties*

### Blackberries

There are trailing, semitrailing, and erect types of blackberries. Trailing types are thorny, semitrailing are thornless, and erect types can be either thorny or thornless. It doesn't necessarily matter which type of blackberry you get, as long as it is suitable for your growing zone. It will come in handy to know which type you have when it comes to plant care, though. Whether a plant is trailing or semitrailing will determine the type of staking and training. Whether it bears fruit on first year or second year growth will affect when you prune the plant.

'Triple Crown' is a semitrailing type suitable to the Mid-Atlantic. 'Chester' is a trailing type that produces lots of fruit. 'Arapaho' is a popular erect type that grows well in the Mid-Atlantic.

You can purchase both container-grown and bare-root plants. If container-grown plants are available in your area, spend the extra money for them. They'll establish themselves better and faster and will be healthier in the long run.

### Raspberries

Raspberries produce fruit in the fall on first year growth (primocanes) or in the summer on second-year growth.

**Fall-bearing varieties:** 'Autumn Bliss', 'Autumn Britten', 'Caroline', 'Dinkum', 'Heritage'.
**Summer-bearing varieties:** 'Boyne', 'Canby', 'Killarney', 'Latham', 'Nova', 'Titan'.

## Trellising Systems for Trailing and Erect Blackberry Types

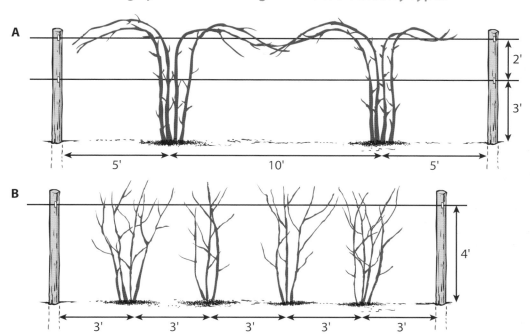

(A) Train trailing plants to a two-wire trellis. (B) Train erect blackberry plants to a one-wire trellis. Note that trailing blackberries need more space between plants than erect blackberries.

Train raspberries the way you'd train erect blackberries. You can let raspberries grow into large clumps, but those become hard to maintain. It's much easier to grow the plants in a single line and train them to a two wire trellis. That way you can easily cut back the older canes and allow new ones to grow.

## ■ Planting

Plant blackberries and raspberries in full sun in well-draining soil with a pH of 5.5 to 6.5. Sun is important for growth and fruit production. Some fruits will produce in partial shade, but bramble berries not only won't produce, but also won't grow.

You can plant container-grown and bare-root plants at any point in the year, as long as snow isn't on the ground and the ground isn't frozen. Soak the roots of bare-root plants for twenty-four hours before planting. Follow instructions on page 48 for planting bare-root plants.

Plant container-grown plants so that the rootball of the plant is at the same level as, or just slightly higher than, the soil around the planting hole. Don't plant too deep!

Brambles grow best with support. You could stake individual plants or grow them against a fence. The best way to grow them though, is to set up a post and wire system with 2 inch × 4 foot posts and heavy-duty wire.

You can train the plants to grow along the wire, and you can anchor the stems using coated tomato wire or twist ties. (I leave several twist ties on the wires so that there's one handy if I happen to decide to go outside and check the blackberries. At the end of the season, I cut the old canes and refasten the twist ties so that they're handy again in spring.)

## Maintenance

**Water:** Frequent watering during the first year is the best way to make sure the plants get off to a good start. Run soaker hoses along the plants (taking care to keep the hoses from touching the stems). Water every two or three days during the first growing season. In subsequent years, watering at least twice a week, giving the plants 1 inch of water per week, will help the plants produce a big crop of fruits for harvest.

**Fertilizer:** Fertilize in spring with a balanced fertilizer.

**Pruning:** Improper pruning of blackberries resulting in no fruit production has broken many a heart. Blackberry stems are called canes. A first-year cane is called a primocane. A second-year cane is called a floricane. Summer-bearing blackberries only bear fruit on second-year floricanes. Fall-bearing blackberries bear fruit on primocanes.

You won't hurt fruit production in your plants if you follow this rule: only prune blackberries all the way to the ground in fall, and only cut down canes that bore fruit during that year. Whether you have

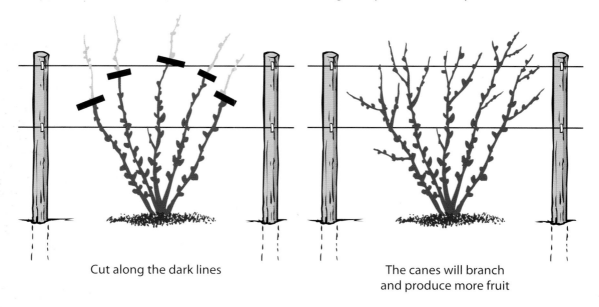

Cut along the dark lines

The canes will branch
and produce more fruit

If you cut off the top 6 to 12 inches of the canes during the first year, the plants will produce side branches that bear fruit during the second year.

plants that bloom on first-year canes or second-year canes, if you only prune the canes that bore fruit, and you only prune in fall, you won't cut down fruit-bearing canes before their time.

The floricanes of summer-bearing blackberries usually start to die back after you pick the fruits, anyway, which makes it easy to see which ones to cut down.

Another type of pruning is pruning to produce more productive side shoots. Prune blackberries back by 6 inches in the middle of summer. This will encourage the plants to produce more side shoots off the main canes, which will result in a bigger fruit crop during the second year.

Prune raspberries by removing the fruiting branches in the summer after the second crop of fruit. You can also prune back the tips of second year branches by 6 inches in the spring to encourage side shoots to grow.

## ▌ *Pest Problems*

Blackberries and raspberries have few pests that are a major problem in the home garden. There are a few diseases that affect plants, including rosette disease. Plant resistant varieties to avoid this problem.

Cane borers attack blackberries. You will be able to tell if you have these insects if the top of a first-year cane wilts and falls over suddenly. Cut below the wilted area and discard the branch with the borer. (Do not compost.)

Occasionally birds will eat your blackberries before you can. If this is a problem, purchase bird netting at a garden center or home-improvement store, and throw the nets over the plants.

## ▌ *Harvesting*

Harvest blackberries when they easily come off the plants. Plants will produce ripe berries for several weeks. Harvest only what you want to eat, and harvest fresh daily.

Raspberries can be grown in the cooler areas of the Mid-Atlantic.

Grape vines need to have support in the garden, but they are well worth the extra effort.

# VINING & GARDEN FRUITS

After covering fruit and nut trees, and shrubby fruits, what's left? Vining fruits and garden fruits. Vining fruits such as grapes are perennial fruits with sprawling growth habits. Melons are similarly sprawling, but are annuals. Strawberries are somewhat in a category of their own—they can be grown as perennials or annuals. Melons and strawberries could be covered in the "vegetables" section, but they're sweet, and we treat them as fruits in the kitchen.

This category of fruits includes plants that can be somewhat tricky to site in the garden. They all take up a fair amount of space, and all but melons are perennial. The question to ask yourself before deciding to grow any of these fruits is, how badly do you want your own?

To get enough strawberries to make a difference on your table, you have to plant a lot of plants, and that takes space. Melons take up a huge amount of space and are susceptible to a number of pests and diseases. I'm not trying to talk you out of growing these, but when it comes to making a real difference in the budget versus taking up a lot of valuable real estate in the garden, these fruits are hogs. Strawberries and melons are cheap to get at the farmers' market when they're in season. If you are low on space, consider growing a few plants for fun but leaving the heavy lifting to market growers in your area.

Fresh strawberries have the best taste, but they can take up a lot of room in the garden.

# GRAPE *(Vitis vinifera)*

Grapes are another fairly easy plant to grow in the home garden. American Bunch Grapes are the types most-suited to Mid-Atlantic Gardens. The ever-popular Concord grape is a bunch grape that is tasty for eating and great for making juice and jelly. You can grow several different types of grapes for different colors and flavors on the table or in your lunch box.

## ■ Recommended Varieties

Here are some of the most highly recommended bunch grapes for Mid-Atlantic gardeners.

**'Himrod':** Golden yellow grape
**'Delaware':** Red grape, great for winemaking.
**'Concord':** Blue/black grape, better for cooler climates.
**'Steuben':** Another blue/black grape that ripens a week after Concord. Sweet/spicy flavor.
**'Niagara':** White grape. Great for snacking.
**'Mars Seedless':** Resistant to many diseases.

Grow grapes for both eating and juice or jelly.

## ■ Planting

You can buy bare-root grapes and container-grown grapes. Plant bare-root grapes in late February to late March. Plant container-grown grapes at any point during the year.

Plant grapes in full sun in well-drained soil high in organic matter. Grapes do not grow well in heavy clay soils or soils where water sits for more than a few hours at a time.

Grapes require support. If you don't want to start over every couple of years, it is best to go big or go home. A post and wire system like you'd use for blackberries will work well for grapes. Situate the wire at a height that's comfortable for you to reach—between waist and chest high works well. Plant grapes with 10 to 20 feet of space between each vine.

## ◼ *Maintenance*

**Water:** Water grapes several times a week as they are becoming established. In subsequent years, give vines 1 inch of water per week during the fruiting season.

**Fertilizer:** Grapes benefit from the application of 2 ounces of ammonium nitrate per vine, spread on the ground in a 2-to-3-foot-diameter area around the trunk. Fertilize in March, May, and July.

Grapes are sensitive to magnesium levels in the soil. If you see yellowing in the spaces between veins of older leaves, there's probably a magnesium shortage. Spread Epsom salts in the same diameter area you'd spread fertilizer at a rate of 2 to 4 ounces per plant to correct this problem.

**Pruning:** The biggest mystery of grape production is pruning. Grape vines have a central stem, called the trunk, and two side shoots called cordons. The plants will bear fruit from the cordons on compressed side shoots called spurs. Each cordon will have many spurs. From the spurs grow shoots with buds that will sprout and produce grapes.

Train new grape vines by allowing them to grow up toward the wire of the trellis. Cut off side shoots while the vine is growing up. Once the vine has reached the wire, cut off the growing tip to force side shoots to grow. Two of these will become the right and left arms of the cordon.

Prune grapes in winter. At each spur, prune back all growths except for one piece of fruiting spur from the previous year's growth. Each fruiting spur should be about 4 inches long and have three to five buds on it.

To keep new fruiting spurs forming, each year remove every other spur down to the cordon. New spurs will sprout.

It's important to know that grapes bear fruit on one-year-old spur growth, so you don't want to cut off that growth when pruning.

## ◼ *Pest Problems*

There are some fungal diseases that affect grapes. Check with your cooperative extension for information about treating fungal diseases.

## ◼ *Harvesting*

Ripe grapes will easily come off in your hand. You can cut individual clusters as they ripen. Do a taste test to see if the grapes are ready to eat!

Melons can take up a lot of space in the garden, but they're fun to grow.

# MELON Watermelon *(Citrullus lanatus)*; Cantaloupe and Honeydew *(Cucumis melo)*

Melons are annual vines related to cucumbers and squash. As such, they are susceptible to all of the pests that plague squashes. If you're limited on space in the vegetable garden, skip the melons and buy them at the farmers' market. If you have space, give them a shot. It's fun to go out into the garden and find tiny watermelons growing larger each day.

## ■ *Recommended Varieties*

**Watermelon:** 'Charleston Gray', 'Crimson Sweet', 'Golden Crown', 'Royal Sweet', 'Tiger Baby'.

**Cantaloupe:** 'Burpee Hybrid', 'Ambrosia', 'Park's Whopper', 'Scoop II'.

**Honeydew:** 'Earlidew'.

## ■ *Planting*

Direct-sow melon seeds in the soil when soil temperatures are at least 65°F. If the soil's not warm, the plants won't grow. These plant require a long growing season, so you might want to start them indoors. They don't transplant well, though, so plant them in peat pots or biodegradable pots that can be directly planted into the garden.

Melons need full sun and rich soil full of compost in order to produce well. The soil pH should be 6.5 to 7.0. If it's any lower, the plants can suffer from calcium deficiencies. Plant seeds in hills at least 4 feet apart, and plant three seeds per hill. Thin plants to one plant every 4 feet after they grow three sets of leaves.

## ■ Maintenance

**Water:** Melons are heavy drinkers. Lay soaker hoses after the plants have sprouted, and water every other day during the growing season. Avoiding overhead watering can prevent some disease problems.

**Fertilizer:** Sidedress with calcium nitrate or composted chicken manure when the vines are 3 feet long.

**Pollination:** Melon plants have both male and female flowers. The flowers have to be pollinated in order to produce fruits. If you want to be absolutely sure that plants have been pollinated, you can hand-pollinate them. Move pollen from a male flower to a female flower using a paintbrush or cotton swab. (Female flowers have a small swelling behind the flower, which is what will grow into the melon.)

## ■ Pest Problems

Melons suffer from the same types of pests that all squash-family plants encounter. Cucumber beetles, flea beetles, squash bugs, and squash vine borers are some of the worst. Use row covers to prevent flying insects from landing on the plants. Lift the row covers for two hours in the morning twice a week to encourage pollination, or hand-pollinate. If you have bad problems with squash bugs and squash vine borers, you might consider growing melons under cover for their entire growing season and hand-pollinating to ensure fruit set.

## ■ Harvesting

When are melons ripe? That is the hardest thing to learn and something you'll figure out over time. Cantaloupe varieties will be ready to harvest around 30 to 35 days after flowering; they should smell sweet. Honeydews take about 40 to 45 days after flowering before they're ready to harvest; they turn pale green.

Watermelons take longer, but the time to maturity differs greatly, depending on the type of melon. Check the seed packet for information about the number of days from planting to harvest or from flowering to harvest. You can tell if watermelons are ripe by looking at the tendril closest to the fruit. When that turns brown, the melons are ready to pick.

# RHUBARB *(Rheum rhabarbarum)*

If you ever read the Little House on the Prairie book *The First Four Years*, which details the first years of Laura Ingalls' marriage to Almanzo Wilder, you'll recall a scene in which the newly married Laura makes a pie for the farmhands using "pie plant." She forgets to add sugar and the pie is so sour that it is inedible. "Pie plant" is rhubarb. You eat the petioles (leaf stems) of this plant, and nothing else. Though it is really a vegetable, it is used in the kitchen as a fruit. Be careful with rhubarb. ONLY the stems are edible after cooking. The rest of the plant is poisonous.

## ■ Recommended Varieties

Plant whatever you can find. It is easier to grow rhubarb from crowns (the roots of one-year-old plants) than it is to grow from seed.

Rhubarb stalks can be green or red, depending on the variety you plant.

**GROWING TIPS**

At some point during the spring or early summer, your rhubarb plants might begin to flower, or "bolt." Cut off this flower stalk as soon as you see it and keep harvesting. Even if the stalk appears after harvest, you still want to cut it off, as leaving it will cause the plant to divert energy to producing seeds, not storing energy in the roots for the next year.

## ■ *When and Where to Plant*

**Temperature:** Not all regions can grow rhubarb. It requires temperatures below 40°F in the winter to break dormancy and temperatures below 75°F to grow well during the summer and replenish its stores for winter growth. Plant in the spring or the fall while the crowns are still dormant.

**Soil:** Rhubarb grows best in loose, well-drained soil with a neutral pH.

**Sun:** Full sun.

## ■ *How to Plant*

**Starting seeds indoors:** Not recommended.

**Planting outside:** Cultivate the soil to a depth of 8 to 10 inches. Plant rhubarb crowns 24 inches apart, covering them with just 1 to 2 inches of soil. Water well.

## ■ *How to Grow*

**Water:** Water rhubarb with the same frequency you'd water sugar snap peas, which is to say regularly, but don't let the soil stay soggy.

**Fertilizer:** Fertilize after harvest with liquid fish emulsion.

**Pest control:** Rhubarb has few pest problems.

## ■ *How to Harvest*

Harvest during the third season of growth. Use a knife to cut off the stalks at the base of the plant. Never remove more than one-third of the plant at any given time. Stop cutting stalks when they are less than ½ inch wide. Let the plant keep growing to produce reserves to allow it sprout next year. Do not eat the leaves!

# STRAWBERRY *(Fragaria × ananassa)*

Warm, fully ripe, fresh-picked strawberries are one of the most delicious things you can eat. Strawberries can be grown as annuals—replanted each fall for fruiting in spring—or as perennials via the mat and row system. If your plants grow well when left in the ground for several years, it is absolutely easier to treat them as perennials. If anthracnose is a problem and plants decline or don't fruit, switch to the annual system of fall planting and spring harvesting.

## ◼ *Recommended Varieties*

There are short-day (June-bearing) strawberries and day-neutral (everbearing) strawberries. Short-day varieties of strawberries do best in the Mid-Atlantic. As with many fruit crops, it is best to purchase plants from local growers. If you have u-pick farms in your area, check them out. They will often have plants for sale.

Because of the number of diseases that affect strawberries, buy resistant varieties when possible.

Use nets to ensure you'll get to eat your strawberries before the birds do.

**'Allstar':** Resistant to red stele and verticillium wilt and have some resistance to leaf scorch and powdery mildew.
**'Delite':** Resistant to both red stele and verticillium wilt.
**'Delmarvel':** Good disease resistance and winter hardiness.
Superior flavor varieties include Redchief, Lateglow, and Sunrise.

## ◼ *Planting*

Strawberries have an unusual growth cycle. For success growing them at home, you need to understand the growth cycle and plant accordingly.

Strawberry plants produce runners during summer. In fall, the plants stop spreading out and flower buds form in the crown of the plant (the center of the plant—a compressed stem). In early spring, the crown sprouts leaves and flowers. Berries form four to five weeks after the flowers open. It takes about three weeks for berries to ripen. When the days grow longer and the temperature warms, plants send out runners again.

Strawberries grow best in full sun in well-drained sandy soils with a pH of 6.0 to 6.5. They do not tolerate heavy clay soils or swampy, poorly drained soils very well.

To grow plants as perennials, plant strawberries 1 foot apart in 4-foot blocks with 2 feet between rows. Cut off any runners that form, so that the plant channels all of its energy into forming healthy crowns.

You can plant new strawberries in spring and allow them to send out runners throughout summer that will bloom and fruit the following year.

If anthracnose is a problem, dig up plants after harvesting, and plant new plants each fall.

## Maintenance

**Water:** Strawberries require extra water at very specific times during their growth cycle:

- Right after planting
- During peak harvest
- After peak harvest when you're encouraging new runners
- In fall when fruit buds for the following year are forming

During these times, water the plants so that the soil is wet to a depth of 6 to 8 inches.

**Mulch:** All strawberries do best when mulched to conserve moisture, and keep weeds under control.

**Fertilizer:** Apply ammonium nitrate (33-0-0) or chicken manure at a rate of 1½ pounds per 100 feet of row from mid-August through mid-September.

## Pest Problems

There are numerous pests and diseases that affect strawberries. Birds are the worst animal pests. Use nets to keep the birds from eating the fruits as they ripen. Multiple fungal and bacterial problems attack strawberry plants. If you think your plants could be afflicted, the best thing to do is to dig up a plant and take it to your county extension service for help with diagnosis and treatment solutions.

## Harvesting

Harvest when the fruits are colorful and can be easily pulled off the plant.

# CHAPTER 8

# VEGETABLE & HERB GARDENING

The fact that homegrown tomatoes taste better than store-bought tomatoes is not only a cliché—it's true. Why? Because when you can pick your produce right before you use it, as opposed to a month before it's going to be used, you can let the fruits develop to their full ripeness and sweetness. You can also grow more varieties that don't have to withstand shipping and warehousing.

Growing herbs in a small kitchen garden makes it more likely that you'll use them.

## Vegetable Gardening Throughout the Year

In the Mid-Atlantic, there are cool seasons and a warm season for gardening. When the seasons are depends on where you live. Different plants grow during warm and cool seasons. The key to successful vegetable gardening is planting the right plant at the right time of year so that you get the biggest harvest the first time around.

In some areas of the Mid-Atlantic, some vegetables traditionally thought of as "cool season" will grow throughout the summer. In the Mountain and Plateau region, kale, Swiss chard, broccoli, and carrots will grow throughout the summer. In these regions, the key to getting the seasons right is planting warm-weather veggies

## Garden Seasons in the Mid-Atlantic

| REGION | Jan. | Feb. | Mar. | Apr. | May | June | July | Aug. | Sept. | Oct. | Nov. | Dec. |
|---|---|---|---|---|---|---|---|---|---|---|---|---|
| Coastal Plain | Cool Season | | | | Warm Season | | | | | Cool Season | | |
| Interior Foothills | | | Cool Season | | Warm Season | | | | | Cool Season | | |
| Piedmont | | | Cool Season | | Warm Season | | | | | Cool Season | | |
| Mountains | | | Cool Season | | | Warm Season | | | Cool Season | | | |
| Plateau | | | Cool Season | | | Warm Season | | | Cool Season | | | |

at the right time. (When the soil has warmed up, and not too early!) In the Coastal Plain, cool-season vegetables will grow from October through April. The Interior Foothills region has a longer cool season than the Mountains and Plateau, as well.

Does all of this seem confusing? Here are two simple tips to plant at the right time.

- Plant warm-season vegetables when the soil temperature is at least 60°F (65°F to 70°F is even better!).
- Plant cool-season vegetables in the spring when soil temperatures are at least 45°F, and the ground has thawed. Plant the vegetables for a fall harvest by seed in August in all areas or as transplants when nighttime air temperatures are regularly below 60°F.

The vegetable and herb profiles in this book are organized to help you distinguish cool and warm-season vegetables so there is no question in your mind as to what you should be planting when.

## Transitioning between Warm- and Cool-Season Gardening

It's easier to transition a vegetable garden between seasons if it is planted in rows. If you plant in rows, you can easily save part of the garden for the next season. Or you can neatly pull up all of one crop and plant another.

Raised beds and small-space gardens can be more challenging. You have to find ways to shoehorn in the new crop while the old crop is finishing up. If you're like me, and you plant the same kind of vegetable in different parts of the garden (I do it partially to thwart pests and partially because I'm disorganized), you can end up with small spaces all over the garden. You'll find yourself wandering around trying to decide what to plant where, not wanting to leave any of the valuable and limited space empty.

A little bit of planning goes a long way when making the transition. If you have the time, patience, and organizational skills to do this, sit down with some pieces of paper and make a grid that shows your garden. With a colored pencil, write in the cool-season plants you plan to grow. In a different-colored pencil, write the warm-season plants that you're planning to plant when the cool-season vegetables are finished. This small bit of organization will also help you keep yourself from going crazy when you go plant shopping—you'll have a better idea of what is going in which space.

This planning is even more important in cooler areas, as you'll be growing most of your vegetables to harvest at the same time, even though you might plant some of them earlier than others.

## Small-Space Vegetable Gardening

Don't say no to edibles, even if you have only a small amount of space in the sun. It's easier than ever to grow enough vegetables to supplement your diet. Raised-bed kits, self-watering containers, and vertical-gardening assemblies allow you to grow vegetables anywhere, with any amount of space. In the Mid-Atlantic, growing in raised beds or containers lets you more easily control the quality of the soil. Whether you deal with sand or clay, poor-draining muck or alkaline rocky soils, raised beds will make your gardening work easier.

## Find Your Favorite Vegetables and Herbs

Ready to get growing? Use this mini-index to find the edibles you want to learn about.

You can see the rows of newly planted seeds delineated by the lighter-colored seed-starting mix covering the seeds.

# Cool-Season Gardening Tips & Tricks

The cool season of vegetable gardening can run all winter or bookend the summer. Some plants, when planted in fall, can be harvested through spring. Others require two different plantings in order to get a continuous harvest. This is noted in individual plant descriptions where applicable.

To heap even more confusion onto the plate, if you want to grow some cool-season vegetables from seeds sown directly into the garden in fall, you will actually sow the seeds in August or September—when your tomatoes are still producing and you're technically still in the "warm season."

Certain plants can sprout from seed when soil temperatures are relatively high (75°F to 85°F) but will grow best when air temperatures start to cool down. Broccoli, cabbage, kale, and many other members of

131

the cabbage family are like this. You will sow these plants outside in late summer, but they will grow and mature during the true cool season. If you grow these plants from transplants, you'll plant out later in the year or early in spring to take advantage of cool weather.

Plants listed in the cool-season section of this book grow best and mature during cooler parts of the year. Most won't grow, other than to germinate, when the weather is too warm. Most of the vegetables in the cool-season vegetable garden palette are originally from northern sections of eastern Europe and thus are well adapted to cool, humid weather.

### Planting Seeds Outside

Many of the cool-season vegetables are easy to grow from seeds planted directly into the garden. This is indicated in the individual plant profiles.

Follow the instructions on the seed packets and in the plant profiles regarding the planting depth. Some seeds, such as peas, need to be planted fairly deep, while others, such as lettuce, barely need to be covered.

Use seed-starting mix instead of regular garden soil. This lightweight mix makes it easy for sprouting seedlings to break out above the soil.

Keep seeds moist while they are sprouting. Established plants can deal with a bit of drought or water fluctuations, but seeds must stay evenly moist while sprouting.

### Planting Transplants

Some plants are much easier to grow from transplants—particularly January–March. The cooler soil temperatures of late winter and early spring cause seeds to take longer to germinate. During that time, they're more susceptible to fungal problems.

Always harden off transplants before planting outside—even if you bought them at a garden center. Hardening off is the process of getting plants used to outdoor conditions, including sun, temperature, and wind. Start by putting your transplants on a porch or sheltered location for about a week. Then move them to a less protected area for another week. Then, plant in the garden bed.

Plant transplants at the recommended finished spacing for the mature plants. Transplants are expensive! You don't want to lose money by having to "thin" transplants later.

### Planning for a Continual Harvest

Succession planting is the process of planting the same plant, several weeks apart, several times throughout the growing season. Lettuce, carrots, radishes, and turnips are examples of plants that you can plant in succession. These vegetables are quick to mature. By planting several crops of these vegetables on a staggered schedule, you ensure a bountiful harvest of fresh produce throughout the growing season. If a vegetable is a good candidate for succession planting, this is indicated in the plant profile.

## Harvesting

In warmer areas of the Mid-Atlantic (Coastal Plain and southern Piedmont/ Foothills regions) you can plant certain vegetables in the fall and harvest throughout the winter. Carrots and kale are two examples of this. The garden bed acts as a sort of "cold storage." Soil conditions during winter are much like a refrigerator: cool with medium humidity. If you want smaller carrots, planting a few successive rows will keep you going for longer, and you can basically use the garden bed as a "storage area" for the harvest. This also works for parsnips. This technique won't work in areas colder than zone 7.

Other vegetables can be harvested at any point during their growth cycle. Turnips and beets, for example, taste just as good when harvested at 1 inch in diameter as they do when harvested at 3 inches. You can't leave them in the ground, but by planting successive rounds of seeds, you can harvest all winter, at various stages of the growth cycle.

Still other plants have to be harvested when they're ready—there's no early harvesting or "cold storage." Cabbage, broccoli, and cauliflower are done when they're done and need to be picked and eaten.

Over time, you will get the hang of which vegetables can stay in the garden until you're ready for them, which ones can be eaten early, and which ones you need to harvest at a specific point in the growth cycle.

## Cover Cropping

If you don't plant the entire garden with cool-season vegetables, consider cover cropping. This is the practice of planting a nitrogen-fixing legume such as winter rye, cereal rye, fava beans, or peas in a section of the garden that you're not using. You will let these plants grow until they are about to flower. Then, cut them down and turn them under into the soil as a "green manure." Cover cropping is an inexpensive way to add nutrients into the soil while preventing erosion from wind or water during winter.

## Crop Rotation

Certain plants in the cool season vegetable garden are highly susceptible to soil-borne diseases. Changing where you plant these plants from season to season helps avoid those problems. This isn't always an option with smaller gardens, though. Cabbage-family plants, including broccoli, cauliflower, collards, kale, and cabbage, are the ones that have the most problems with soil diseases and fungi. If you find yourself facing problems with diseases of the soil, consider growing just those crops in containers with new soil each season.

# ARUGULA *(Eruca sativa)*

Arugula is an annual green that thrives during cool weather but that will also survive our warm and humid summers as long as it is watered regularly. Summer-grown arugula has a wasabi-hot flavor—different than the milder winter greens. Arugula is hardy to temperatures around 20°F, which means you need to have some frost cloth handy if the forecast is for colder weather. Once the plants start to bolt (send up flower stalks), they're nearing the end of their life cycle. You can cut off the stalks to prolong leaf production, but eventually it's better to move on to harvesting from newer plantings.

## ■ Recommended Varieties

The straight species of salad arugula grows fine in the Mid-Atlantic. The salad arugula variety 'Astro' is heat tolerant, a plus for our region. Wild arugula (*Diplotaxis tenuifolia*) is a type of arugula with longer, more deeply incised (cut) leaves. It is spicier than salad arugula.

## ■ When and Where to Plant

**Temperature:** Arugula grows best in cool weather. Plant outside and grow year-round in the Coastal Plain. In the interior foothills, grow arugula from March through June and again in August through October. In the Plateau and Mountains, plant outside in April and harvest through early October.

**Soil:** Plants thrive in deep, fertile soil with lots of organic matter. The best pH is 6.0 to 6.8.

**Sun:** Full sun to partial shade.

## ■ How to Plant

**Starting seeds indoors:** You can start seeds indoors year-round if you prefer working with transplants in the garden bed. You do not need a heat mat, as arugula prefers cooler temperatures.

**Planting outside:** Soak the seeds overnight before planting outside for faster germination.

## ■ How to Grow

**Water:** Arugula needs steady moisture, particularly as the weather warms, to keep it from bolting.

**Fertilizer:** Sidedress with a balanced fertilizer (10-10-10, for example) once a month to encourage steady leaf production.

**Pest control:** Flea beetles are the most common pest to strike arugula. Use floating row covers to control these pests when they are active.

**GROWING TIPS**

For milder leaves in summer, provide arugula plants with some shade.

To keep pests away from arugula, plant away from cabbage-family plants (which harbor the same pests).

## ■ *When and How to Harvest*

Arugula is cut and come again. Young leaves are tender and mild, while older leaves are spicier and better for braising. Use scissors to cut the leaves at the base of the plant. Do not pull up the entire plant.

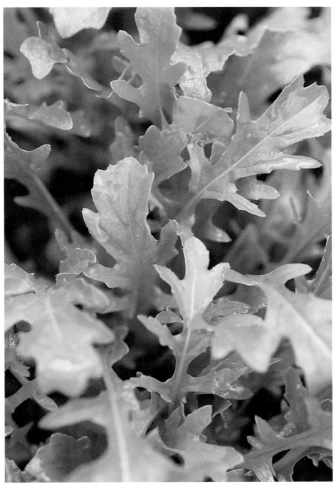

Mix arugula in with other salad greens.

# ASPARAGUS *(Asparagus officinalis)*

Asparagus is a long-lived perennial vegetable that tastes 100 percent better when you can grow and harvest it yourself than when you buy it at the grocery store. The most difficult aspect of growing asparagus for most people is patience. You have to wait at least three years from the time you plant to when you can harvest. It's worth the wait, though, if you have an area where you can plant asparagus crowns and leave them alone to grow.

## ■ Recommended Varieties

Plant all-male varieties Jersey Giant, Jersey Prince, and Jersey Knight. You'll buy asparagus "crowns," which are the roots of one-year-old plants. Starting with crowns and not seeds cuts down on the length of time from planting to harvest. (If you start from seed, it takes four years for the plants to grow large enough for you to harvest.)

## ■ When and Where to Plant

**Temperature:** Plant asparagus crowns when the soil has warmed to a temperature of at least 50°F. (Timing varies by region.) If planted when the soil is any cooler, the plants can succumb to crown rot.

**Soil:** Asparagus plants grow best in a loose, well-drained soil with a pH of 6.5 to 7.5 (slightly higher than some plants).

**Sun:** Full sun.

## ■ How to Plant

**Starting seeds indoors:** Not recommended.

**Planting outside:** Dig a furrow or trench that is 6 inches deep. Amend the trench with 0-20-0 fertilizer to help the plants become established. Place the crowns 12 inches apart in the furrow and then cover and water. Space rows 1 to 2 feet apart.

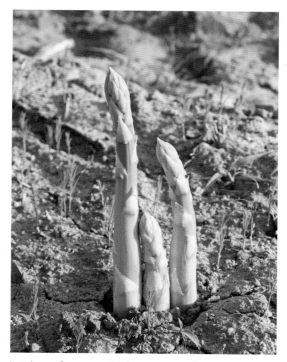

It takes a few years before you can harvest asparagus, but the results are worth the wait.

## ■ *How to Grow*

**Water:** Asparagus plants are fairly drought tolerant, but they will need to be watered with about the same frequency that you would water a new tree or shrub (once or twice a week) while they're getting established. After the first season, water once a week if your area sees no measurable precipitation. Do not overwater! The roots of the plant don't like to sit in wet soil!

**Fertilizer:** Fertilize at the time of planting with 0-20-0 fertilizer. Fertilize plants with composted chicken manure at the end of the harvest season (mid-summer) to encourage good growth and storage for the next year's harvest.

**Pest control:** Asparagus has few pest problems.

## ■ *How to Harvest*

Harvest during the third season of growth. (After the plant is two years old.) The asparagus shoots will start to emerge once the soil warms up to about 50°F. Harvest 6-inch spears by snapping them off at the base of the soil. Harvest two to four times a week. Once the spears start to be less than ⅜ inch in diameter, stop harvesting and let the spears grow into ferns. This growth will photosynthesize and produce energy for the next year.

**GROWING TIPS**

It is an old wives' tale that you should use salt as a weed control with asparagus. It is never a good idea to throw salt in the garden! Cultivate around asparagus plants during the first year to reduce weed problems. You can use pre-emergent herbicides during the second year if you have big weed problems. Mulch is also useful when growing asparagus.

Let the tops of the plants grow throughout the summer. Do not cut back the tops until the following spring when you see new shoots.

# BEET *(Beta vulgaris)*

Beets are primarily a root crop, but their tops—or leaves, which are also called beet greens—are tasty and nutritious, too. Young greens (or tops) are great in salads, while the larger greens you get when harvesting beets taste good when braised and tossed with pasta. Beets need full sun and loose soil to form good roots. As with all root crops, beets grow best when sown directly into the garden, rather than planted as transplants. If your only experience with beets is pickled varieties on the salad bar, you're missing out. Beets taste delicious when roasted. You can also grate raw beets onto your salads. In addition to red varieties, you can also grow white, yellow, and striped varieties.

## Recommended Varieties

The following red varieties grow well in the Mid-Atlantic. 'Kestrel', 'Red Cloud', 'Red Ace', 'Ruby Queen', 'Frono', Detroit Dark Red strains, and 'Rodina'. 'Golden' is a yellow variety. 'Chioggia' is a red-and-white-striped variety.

## When and Where to Plant

**Temperature:** Beets germinate best when soil temperatures are 55°F to 75°F. The plants grow best when air temperatures are 60°F to 65°F. In the Mountain and Plateau regions, sow seeds outside April 15 to June 1

Both the tops and the roots of beets can be eaten.

and again August 1 to 15. In the Coastal Plain and southern Piedmont, sow seeds outside in February and March and again in September.

**Soil:** Beets need deep, loose, fertile soils with a pH of 5.8 to 7.0.

**Sun:** Full sun.

**Starting seeds indoors:** Not recommended.

**Planting outside:** Sow seeds outside 2 inches apart and ½ inch deep.

## How to Grow

**Water:** Beets need even moisture to avoid scab, a condition in which brown, raised patches form on the outsides of the roots.

**Fertilizer:** Use a balanced fertilizer when planting, and follow up with a low-nitrogen, high-phosphorus fertilizer when the tops are 4 inches tall.

**Pest control:** Cercospora leaf spot is a fungus that causes brown scabby spots on leaves and interferes with sugar production and root development. Plant resistant varieties if disease becomes a problem in your garden.

## When and How to Harvest

To harvest beet greens for salads while keeping the roots growing, use scissors to cut no more than one-quarter of the leaves at any time. To grow beets for this dual purpose, it is best to use small beet greens only as an addition to salads, not as the only green in a salad bowl. To check if roots are ready to harvest, pull one up as a test. Remember: plants you grow at home could be different varieties or have had different care than those you see at the grocery store. Just because your beets might be smaller than you expect doesn't mean they aren't ready to eat. Once beets reach their indicated maturity (usually after 60 days growing), it's best to harvest. If you leave them in the ground, they'll become woody and unpleasant to eat.

**GROWING TIPS**

Beets will develop internal black spot if boron isn't available in the soil. If this is a problem in your garden, apply borax at a rate of 1 pound per acre at least seven days prior to planting.

Beets planted at the proper time have fewer pest problems than beets planted late. If you're confused about when to plant, err on the side of earlier rather than later.

Newer hybrid varieties are sweeter than older varieties.

# BROCCOLI *(Brassica oleracea,* Italica Group*)*

Broccoli is the go-to vegetable for the dinner table or the picnic basket. Like all vegetables in the cabbage family, broccoli is highly nutritious, because it is filled with vitamins and minerals. Research studies have also shown that broccoli has anticancer properties—when eaten raw. In most of the Mid-Atlantic you have the opportunity to grow multiple crops of broccoli throughout the cool season. (In the Mountain and Plateau regions broccoli is best grown as a spring crop.) Change where you plant broccoli in the garden from year to year to prevent plants from succumbing to soilborne diseases.

## ■ Recommended Varieties

'Packman' and 'Southern Comet' are two varieties that grow best during the early spring season. Both of these varieties produce side shoots after the main head is harvested.

For disease resistance, including head rot and downy mildew, plant the 'Everest' cultivar. (It also works well for a fall harvest.) Other suggested varieties include 'Gypsy', 'Premium Crop' and 'Veronica'.

## ■ When and Where to Plant

**Temperature:** Broccoli germinates best when soil temperatures are 50°F to 85°F. It grows best when air temperatures are in the 60sF. In the Mountain and Plateau areas, plant transplants outside April 1 to 15 in the spring and sow seed for fall harvests in July. In the Coastal Plain and Piedmont regions, plant transplants outside in mid-March for spring harvests and sow seeds outside in mid-August for fall harvests. Plant transplants outside in September for fall harvests.

**Soil:** Soil composition is less important (broccoli will grow equally well in sandy soils or clay-filled soils) than soil pH. The soil pH for broccoli must be 6.0 to 6.5. If the soil pH is lower than 6.0, mix lime into the soil at least two months before planting.

**Sun:** Full sun.

Successive crops of broccoli can be grown throughout the cool season in the Mid-Atlantic.

**GROWING TIPS**

Don't compost broccoli plants—doing so can spread the myriad diseases affecting them to your entire compost pile.

Some varieties of broccoli are extremely temperature sensitive. If there's a cold snap (temperatures of 35°F to 50°F) for more than ten days after broccoli is planted, the plants will bolt (flower) and you won't get a head to harvest. You can try to prevent the cold from affecting the plants by covering them with row covers. Once the plants bolt, you have to just pull them up and start over.

## How to Plant

**Starting seeds indoors:** Start seeds indoors at least 60 days before you want to plant transplants outside. Broccoli takes 3 to 10 days to germinate and about a month to grow to transplantable size.

**Planting outside:** Always harden off your transplants before planting them outside in spring. It is easier to direct-sow a fall crop and get good results than it is to direct-sow a spring crop outside. Go with transplants for spring. Leave 12 to 18 inches between transplants, or thin seedlings to this spacing after direct-seeding.

## How to Grow

**Water:** Keep broccoli evenly moist throughout the growing season.

**Fertilizer:** Add compost to the soil before planting. Then sidedress with calcium nitrate when the plants are 6 inches tall.

**Pest control:** Broccoli and other cabbage-family plants are susceptible to a variety of pests, including aphids, cabbagewhites, cabbage loopers, diamondback moths, flea beetles, harlequin bugs, slugs, and weevils. Plant resistant varieties when possible, and use floating row covers when flying insects are active. Use *B.t.* for caterpillar contraol or Neem oil to control a wide range of pests.

## When and How to Harvest

Cut the center flower head when it is still dark green and tight (about 60 days for most varieties—it will say on the seed packet). When the head starts to loosen and turn yellow, it's too late to harvest. If you're growing a variety that produces side shoots, leave the rest of the plant in the garden for up to two months. If the variety is primarily grown for the large center head, cut the heads and pull up the rest of the plant to make room for other vegetable crops.

# BRUSSELS SPROUTS
### (*Brassica oleracea,* Gemmifera Group)

Brussels sprouts—you love them or you hate them. I love them sautéed with butter and bacon, but that completely defeats the purpose of eating a vegetable. One reason to grow this unusual-looking cabbage-family plant is that it's easy to grow if you can keep the pests away and are patient. Leave Brussels sprouts in the garden until there's a frost, which will make the "sprouts," which look like mini-cabbages, sweeter.

The "sprouts" of Brussels sprouts develop along the plant stem. You harvest from the bottom up.

## ■ *Recommended Varieties*

'Oliver' is a taller variety that produces earlier sprouts. 'Jade Cross' hybrids are dwarf varieties less likely to fall over in the garden. 'Diablo' is another recommended variety.

## ■ *When and Where to Plant*

**Temperature:** Brussels sprouts can start growing in the warmer days of summer but will need cool weather in order to mature. In all areas, sow seed outside in late June. Plant transplants outside in mid-July to early August for a fall harvest.

**Soil:** Add compost to the soil before planting. Brussels sprouts are heavy feeders. Soil pH should be 6.0 to 7.5. Higher pH levels help keep soilborne diseases from affecting the plants.

**Sun:** Full sun.

## ■ *How to Plant*

**Starting seeds indoors:** It takes 30 to 45 days to grow plants inside for transplanting outside. You'll need to harden the plants off before planting outside—the plants need to get used to the heat (for summer plantings) before they go in the garden.

**Planting outside:** Plant transplants outside, 16 to 18 inches apart, or direct-sow into the garden, at 6 inches spacing. Thin seedlings to the 16-inch spacing after plants are 6 inches tall.

## ■ *How to Grow*

**Water:** Keep evenly moist throughout the growing season.

**Fertilizer:** Fertilize with a balanced fertilizer once a month throughout the growing season.

**Pest control:** Cutworms can affect transplants. To protect young plants, wrap the bottom 3 to 4 inches of stem with newspaper or foil. Cabbageworms can attack plant leaves. If you see evidence of cabbageworms, control with *Bacillus thuringiensis* (*B.t.*).

## ■ *When and How to Harvest*

You can start harvesting the sprouts about three months after planting. Sprouts mature from the bottom up. As a sprout begins to form, clip off the leaf below the sprout and let it grow to be ¾ to 1 inch in diameter. Then use clippers to harvest the sprouts as they mature. (You can take enough at a time to eat!)

---

**GROWING TIPS**

Brussels sprouts are shallow rooted and prone to falling over. Stake the taller varieties to keep these plants upright and away from the soil.

If the plant is growing but the sprouts aren't getting any bigger, cut off the top of the plant. This will cause the plant to put more energy into producing the sprouts

# CABBAGE *(Brassica oleracea)*

Cabbage is a classic cool-season vegetable. In warmer areas of the Mid-Atlantic, you can grow it from fall through winter and into spring. In the Mountain and Plateau areas, cabbage is a fall or spring crop. You can't beat it for utility—it is easy to store and can be added to soups, stir-fries, and cold salads. Along with other cruciferous vegetables, cabbage is one of the most nutritious vegetables you can eat.

## ■ *Recommended Varieties*

When selecting seeds or transplants, read the plant tag or description and try to select varieties that are resistant to common cabbage diseases such as fusarium wilt, yellows, and black rot. 'Resistant Golden Acre' is a top performer for spring plantings. 'Early Jersey Wakefield' and 'Savoy Ace' are two tasty white varieties. 'Ruby Ball', 'Red Express', and 'Red Rookie' are three red varieties that do well in this area.

## ■ *When and Where to Plant*

**Temperature:** Cabbage needs soil temperatures of at least 50°F to germinate and air temperatures of 60°F to 65°F. Temperature fluctuations can cause spring plantings to bolt. In the Plateau and Mountain regions plant spring transplants outside from mid-April to early May. If frost is in the forecast, cover the plants. In the Piedmont and Coastal Plain, plant transplants outside in mid-March for a spring harvest. Direct-sow seeds outside in all areas in mid-July for fall harvests. Transplant seedlings outside for fall harvests in mid-August.

**Soil:** Cabbage grows best in well-drained, fertile soil. Add compost before planting. The soil pH needs to be at least 6.0 for cabbage to grow. A pH of 6.5 to 7.2 is even better. If the pH is low, add lime to the soil before planting. Higher-pH soils keep club-root disease at bay.

**Sun:** Full sun.

---

**GROWING TIP**

Rotate the cabbage planting areas in your garden, never replanting in the same place more frequently than every two years. Cabbage plants and other cruciferous vegetables are highly susceptible to diseases that linger in the soil. If you have limited space and plan to grow just a few heads per year, consider making a "cabbage barrel" (a half whiskey barrel planted with cabbage) in which you can replace the soil each time you plant new cabbages.

Cabbage is easy to grow and easy to store.

## How to Plant

**Starting seeds indoors:** Sow seeds inside four to six weeks before you plan to plant outside. Harden off transplants before planting in spring.

**Planting outside:** Because smaller cabbage heads taste better and store more easily, plant cabbage transplants 12 to 18 inches apart in rows 3 feet apart or on 24-inch centers if growing in raised beds. The plants will grow to be 12 to 24 inches in diameter.

## How to Grow

**Water:** Cabbages need evenly moist soil throughout their growing period. Once the heads start to firm up, you can keep the soil on the drier side.

**Fertilizer:** Sidedress with organic, slow-release fertilizer at the time of planting. One month after planting, apply another application.

**Pest control:** Look for caterpillars eating the leaves. (They're most likely to show up in fall and spring—not winter.) If you see them, treat with *Bacillus thuringiensis* (*B.t.*) to control them.

## When and How to Harvest

The part of the cabbage that you harvest is called a head, and smaller heads taste better. Once the head feels firm, it is ready to pick. Use pruners or a knife to cut off the head just below the base. Leave the stem in the ground because you might get a few smaller heads to form. You can "store" cabbages in the garden for a while, but the longer you leave them in the ground, the more you run the risk of the heads becoming fibrous and bitter.

# CARROT *(Daucus carota)*

Once you've eaten a carrot you grew yourself, you will never want to go back to the bland, bitter, soapy-tasting carrots from the grocery store. Carrots actually have flavor, but you'd never know it if you didn't pull one out of your own garden and eat it. These vegetables get a bad rap for being hard to grow. They actually aren't, as long as you prepare the soil well and grow them at the right time of the year. If your garden is sun challenged, you can still grow carrots. They'll produce roots with as little as four hours of sun a day.

## ■ *Recommended Varieties*

For carrots that look like typical carrots, grow 'Danvers Half Long', 'Spartan Bonus', 'Scarlet Nantes', 'Nevis'(heat tolerant), 'Apache', 'Camden', or 'Chantenay'. 'Orlando Gold' is a yellow variety. 'Thumbelina' carrots grow fat and round instead of long and skinny. 'Little Finger' carrots are true "baby" carrots, growing to 4 inches or less. 'Bolero' is a good carrot to plant in the late summer for fall and early winter harvest.

For best results, plant carrots in soil that is loose and free of rocks.

## ■ *When and Where to Plant*

**Temperature:** Carrots will germinate when the soil temperature is 45°F to 85°F. They'll grow best at temperatures of 60°F to 65°F. They can stay in the garden all winter in the Coastal Plain regions and in the garden all summer in the Mountain and Plateau regions. Sow seeds outside February through April and again in August and September in the Coastal Plains region and Piedmont. Sow seeds outside in April or May through June in the Mountain and Plateau areas for a summer harvest and again in August for a fall harvest.

**Soil:** The most important part of growing carrots is the soil. For carrots to grow long, even roots, the soil has to be loose and free of rocks. If you can grow carrots in raised beds, you'll have fewer problems with the soil being too hard or full of things that get in the roots' way. Turn the soil over and work finely sifted compost into it before planting.

**Sun:** Full sun to partial shade.

**GROWING TIPS**

Mix carrot seeds with fine sand to make sowing the seeds easier. Because carrot seeds are so small, it's possible to sow too many in one area and waste seeds. Sowing too many also makes for tedious thinning.

Cover the orange tops of the carrot roots if they start to peek out. Exposure to light will make them turn green or brown.

Don't throw out the little carrots that you pull up when you thin the rows—those are real "baby" carrots! Use them in salads.

Too much nitrogen fertilizer will make carrots grow large tops and small roots.

Carrots don't compete well with weeds, so make sure to pull weeds from around carrots as soon as you see them.

## How to Plant

**Starting seeds indoors:** Not recommended.

**Planting outside:** Cover seeds with seed-starting mix, and keep the seeds moist while germinating. Be patient! It can take up to three weeks for carrots to germinate, and the soil must stay evenly moist the whole time you're waiting.

## How to Grow

**Water:** Keep moist while germinating and evenly watered during the growing season.

**Thinning:** Thin carrots to 1 inch apart after they sprout and the first true leaves (which look like the second set of leaves) appear. When plants are 3 inches tall, thin to 3-inch spacing.

**Fertilizer:** Add compost to the garden before planting.

**Pest control:** Carrots are fairly pest-free in the home garden. The larvae of the swallowtail butterfly will eat the tops sometimes, but this rarely causes enough damage to worry about.

## When and How to Harvest

Carrots take 60 to 75 days to grow to maturity. You can start to harvest them as soon as the roots turn orange (or red or yellow, depending on the variety). Don't let any carrots grow to be larger than 1½ inches wide— they'll start to taste like turpentine at that point. To harvest, just grasp the leafy top and pull. You don't have to harvest every carrot at the same time. Work your way along the row, harvesting what you want to eat at the time of harvest. You can leave carrots in the ground for about a month after they reach full size.

# CAULIFLOWER (*Brassica oleracea,* Botrytis Group)

To get white heads, tie the top of the leaves together over the first small curds.

It's fun to grow your own cauliflower in the garden. It always seems like one day you see nothing but leaves, and you come back the next day to see a cauliflower. It probably isn't that dramatic, but because it takes cauliflowers so long to mature, once you plant them, you tend to ignore them, to some extent. The mature head is somewhat of a surprise. When you think "cauliflower," you probably think of white vegetables, but colored varieties—orange and purple—are available and easier to grow.

## ■ *Recommended Varieties*

'Amazing' takes 68 days to maturity and is both heat and cold tolerant. It grows well in the fall, in particular. 'Snow Crown' is a fast grower (50 days to maturity) that also tolerates swings in the weather. 'Fremont' is self-blanching and does not require tying. 'Graffiti' is a purple type that grows well for fall harvests.

### GROWING TIPS

To get pretty white cauliflower heads, you have to blanch them. Blanching prevents light from reaching the heads, which prevents them from coloring up, hence the term *blanching*, which also means whitening. When the small cauliflower curds begin to form (they will look like baby cauliflowers), use twine to tie the top leaves of the plants together.

Cauliflowers are temperature sensitive. If a cold snap is predicted (temperatures under 50°F for more than ten days in a row), cover the plants with row covers or poly (rolls of clear plastic) to keep the temperature steady. Otherwise, the plants will bolt.

## When and Where to Plant

**Temperature:** Cauliflowers are more sensitive to day/night temperature swings than other plants. In fact, they need cooler nights than days. Seeds will germinate with soil temperatures of 45°F to 85°F. For best growth, daytime temperatures should be 60°F to 70°F and nighttime temperatures 50°F to 60°F. You can sow seeds for fall cauliflower crops directly into the garden in July in all regions of the Mid-Atlantic. For spring crops plant transplants outside in March in the Coastal Plain and Piedmont (cover if frost is in the forecast) and in April in the Mountains and Plateau.

**Soil:** Soil pH is important for cauliflower. The ideal pH is 6.0 to 6.5. Cauliflowers are also heavy feeders, so add compost to the garden before planting.

**Sun:** Full sun.

## How to Plant

**Starting seeds indoors:** It takes a little over a month to grow transplants large enough to plant out in the garden. It's easier to start these plants from seed right in the garden.

**Planting outside:** Sow seeds 4 inches apart and thin to 12 inches apart after the plants have three sets of leaves. Space transplants 12 to 18 inches apart and plant them 2 to 3 inches deeper than the soil line. The stems will elongate as the plants grow.

## How to Grow

**Water:** Keep plants evenly moist throughout the growing season. If plants become stressed because of drought or dry soil, they will bolt and you'll lose the heads.

**Fertilizer:** Cauliflower is a heavy feeder—particularly of nitrogen and potassium. Sidedress with a balanced fertilizer once a month during the growing season or apply a slow release fertilizer at planting time.

**Pest control:** Cauliflower plants are susceptible to the same pests and diseases that afflict all cabbage-family plants. Protect young plants from cutworms by wrapping their stems with newspaper. Cabbage loopers and cabbage-worms attack cauliflower—though less in fall. Keep an eye out for worms. You can use *Bacillus thuringiensis* (*B.t.*) as an organic remedy.

## When and How to Harvest

Check the seed packet or plant tag to determine when your cauliflower plants will be ready for harvest (the number of days from planting to maturity). Once they're ready, pull up the entire plant. Cauliflower heads cannot sit in the garden once they've reached maturity—they'll start to have problems with rot and fungus, and they may bolt.

# COLLARDS *(Brassica oleracea,* Acephala Group*)*

You might think of collards as a Southern vegetable, but they grow just fine in the Mid-Atlantic. This is one of those vegetables that you're more likely to eat if you grow your own. For some reason, fresh-picked collards from the garden seem less stringy and bitter than those you buy at the store. Collards are easy to grow. They're frost tolerant, require no special care (beyond routine pest scouting), and are prolific. Tradition calls for cooking collards in a slow cooker with a ham hock. That's a good way to render their nutritive value null. Try braising collard leaves with garlic, onions, and lemon juice. That's a tastier and healthier way to eat them.

## ■ Recommended Varieties

The best varieties for the Mid-Atlantic include 'Top Bunch', 'Flash', 'Champion', and 'Blue Max'.

## ■ When and Where to Plant

**Temperature:** Seeds will germinate in temperatures of 50°F to 85°F. Direct-sow outside for a fall or winter crop. Sow seeds outside in July for a fall crop and plant transplants in April for a spring-early summer crop in the Plateau and Mountain regions. Sow seeds outside in August or September for a fall and winter crop in the Coastal Plain and Piedmont regions. Plant transplants in March for a spring harvest.

**Soil:** For the biggest plants, add generous amounts of compost or composted manure to the garden before planting collards. Test the pH to make sure it is 6.0 to 6.5. Add lime if necessary to raise the pH.

**Sun:** Full sun to partial shade.

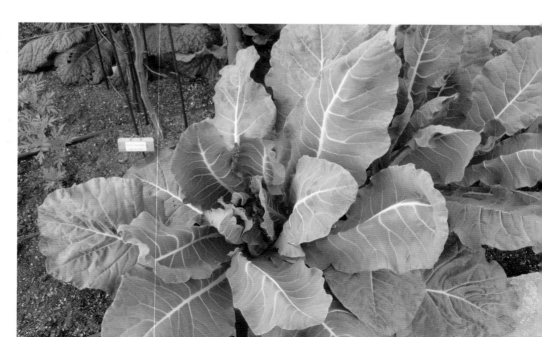

**GROWING TIPS**

As a leafy green, collards are heavy feeders and need a steady supply of nitrogen to keep growing. Sidedress with a high-nitrogen fertilizer every four weeks during the growing season. Composted chicken manure works well on this.

Rotate the planting area for collards and other cabbage-family plants, and try not to plant in the same place more frequently than every three years.

If you direct-sow collards into the garden, you'll have to thin some of the seedlings. Don't throw out these young plants! Add them to salads or stir-fries. Smaller collard leaves aren't stringy.

## How to Plant

**Starting seeds indoors:** It takes six weeks to produce plants large enough to transplant. Decide when you want to plant outside, and start seeds inside accordingly.

**Planting outside:** Sow seeds outside for a fall or winter harvest. Sow seeds 2 inches apart. When plants are 4 to 6 inches tall, thin plants to 24 inches apart.

## How to Grow

**Water:** Keep plants evenly moist, never allowing the soil to completely dry out.

**Fertilizer:** Fertilize every four weeks during the growing season. Mulch with grass clippings and other high-nitrogen materials to encourage steady leaf growth.

**Pest control:** Use floating row covers to cover collard plants when you see white butterflies (cabbagewhites) around the plants. If you see cabbageworms, you can use *Bacillus thuringiensis* (*B.t.*) to control them.

## When and How to Harvest

Harvest individual leaves and allow the plant to keep growing throughout the season. Start by cutting the outermost leaves first, which will keep the plant growing. Once the plant has matured (in 60 to 70 days), you can also cut the entire plant and bring it inside to process. Collards will keep in the refrigerator crisper drawer for a few weeks, but they taste better and have more nutrients when they're eaten soon after harvesting.

Opposite: Collards are easy to grow and good for you!

Once harvested, garlic can be stored in a cool, dry location.

# GARLIC *(Allium sativum)*

Garlic, and lots of it, makes everything taste better! Selecting the right variety makes all the difference, as does planting time. Garlic needs at least 40 days of weather under 40°F for the clove that you plant to split into a bulb with multiple cloves. For this reason, garlic is a fall- and winter-grown vegetable in the Mid-Atlantic. If you can purchase garlic bulbs locally, all the better—you're more likely to have success with your plantings.

## ■ *Recommended Varieties*

There are two types of garlic: softneck and hardneck. Softneck varieties grow best in the warmer areas of the Mid-Atlantic. They do not produce flower stalks, but they are good for braiding, and they store well. Elephant garlic, while not a true garlic, is cultivated the same way that you would cultivate garlic, and it grows well in the entire Mid-Atlantic region. Hardneck garlic varieties produce flower stalks, or scapes, that are good for pickling. They're best for growing in the Mountain and Plateau regions.

Good softneck cultivars to plant in the Piedmont and Coastal Plains include the Creole softneck varieties 'Burgundy' and 'Ajo Rojo'. 'Silverskin' and artichoke types also grow well in the Mid-Atlantic.

Hardneck varieties for the Plateau and Mountain regions include 'Rocambole' and 'German Extra Hardy'.

## ■ When and Where to Plant

**Temperature:** Garlic grows best in cool weather, at temperatures of 50°F to 60°F. Plant garlic bulbs outside in fall. The bulbs will grow throughout the winter and will be ready to harvest in early summer.

**Soil:** The soil pH needs to be 6.0 to 6.8. Add compost to the soil prior to planting. Garlic grows especially well in raised beds. The extra drainage prevents the bulbs from rotting.

**Sun:** Full sun.

## ■ How to Plant

**Starting seeds indoors:** Not recommended.

**Planting outside:** Plant garlic cloves 1 inch deep and 4 inches apart.

## ■ How to Grow

**Water:** Keep the soil moist during the first four weeks after planting—this is when the garlic cloves are growing roots. After that, they do not need extra water until spring. Resume watering once you see leaves start to appear. At the end of the life cycle, decrease watering to allow the bulbs to dry out.

**Fertilizer:** If you added compost to the soil before planting, you do not need to fertilize while the plants are growing. If you didn't add compost, topdress the area where garlic is planted with an organic fertilizer in spring.

**Pest control:** Garlic plants are fairly pest tolerant. In fact, garlic cloves are used in many organic pest control products!

## ■ When and How to Harvest

Garlic is ready to harvest when the tops start dying back. When you see the leaves start to turn yellow, stop watering the bulbs. Once the tops have died back, use a trowel or soil knife to gently dig up the bulbs. (Sometimes you can pull the bulbs up by the leaves, but not always.) You can store garlic by braiding the tops together and hanging in a cool, dry location.

---

### GROWING TIPS

Don't try to plant garlic that you purchase at the grocery store. It might not be the right variety for your area, and it also might have been treated to prevent sprouting.

Keep the garlic patch weeded—garlic bulbs don't compete well with weeds.

# KALE *(Brassica oleracea,* Acephala Group*)*

Kale has become an "it" vegetable. Everyone is drinking kale smoothies, eating kale chips, and generally espousing the benefits of this leafy green vegetable. It's for good reason, though: kale is the most nutrient-dense vegetable per calorie you can eat. It's also easy to grow. Once you plant it, you can basically leave it alone and harvest from the plants for months. Kale even grows through the summer in the Mid-Atlantic. Young leaves are tender enough to put in fresh salads, while larger leaves are perfect for soups and braised greens.

For a tasty and healthy treat, prepare a large bunch of kale by removing the center ribs and tearing the leaves into 1- to 2-inch pieces. Place in a bowl with a sprinkle of salt, a bit of olive oil, and a generous soaking of flavored vinegar. You'll find yourself craving this delicious salad and searching for new flavored vinegars to try it with.

## ■ *Recommended Varieties*

Recommended varieties include 'Green Curled Scotch', 'Early Siberian', 'Vates', 'Dwarf Blue Curled Scotch', and 'Blue Knight'. 'Redbor' is a purple variety with large, curly, purple leaves and veins. 'Red Russian' has green leaves with a red vein. The young leaves of 'Red Russian' are great in salads. 'Toscano' is a dinosaur-type kale (it has wrinkly leaves like wrinkly dinosaur skin).with long, strappy, wrinkly leaves. It holds up well in cooking. Kale is kale, though. Get your hands on some seeds and transplants, plant at the right time, and you're almost guaranteed success.

## ■ *When and Where to Plant*

**Temperature:** Kale seeds will germinate in temperatures of 45°F to 95°F. Kale grows best with daytime temperatures of 60°F to 65°F. You can grow kale through the summer in the entire Mid-Atlantic if you want to. Sow seeds outside in all regions in July for a fall (and winter in some areas) harvest. Plant transplants outside in March and April for growing during the spring and summer.

**Soil:** Add compost to the soil before planting. Test the soil to make sure that the pH is 6.0 to 7.0.

**Sun:** Full sun to partial shade; will last into the summer in partial shade.

## ■ *How to Plant*

**Starting seeds indoors:** Start seeds indoors one month before you want to transplant outdoors.

**Planting outside:** Plant seeds outside 3 inches apart and transplants 8 to 12 inches apart.

## ■ *How to Grow*

**Water:** Keep kale growing, thriving, and producing tender (not bitter and fibrous) leaves by watering consistently when the plants are actively growing.

**Fertilizer:** As with all green, leafy vegetables, kale is a high-nitrogen feeder. Fertilize by sidedressing with an organic, slow-release fertilizer every three to four weeks during the growing season.

**Pest control:** Kale is much hardier and much more resistant to pests than most other plants in the cabbage family. Aphids can be a problem. Control these with insecticidal soap. Cabbageworms and cabbage loopers can also munch on kale. If you see the worms, treat with *Bacillus thuringiensis* (*B.t.*).

**GROWING TIP**

Kale tastes better when harvested in spring or fall. You can keep plants growing through summer, but wait for cooler weather to arrive before resuming harvesting.

## ■ *When and How to Harvest*

Keep your scissors handy when harvesting kale. A sharp yank can cause the whole plant to come out of the ground. Cut small young leaves (1 inch long or less) to use in fresh salads. Harvest the larger leaves from the bottom of the plant up. This lets inner leaves keep growing. You'll know when it's time to stop harvesting by the taste of the leaves. When they get to be too stringy or woody, dig the plants up and make room for something else.

Kale is easy to grow and a popular edible.

# KOHLRABI *(Brassica oleracea,* Gongylodes Group*)*

The stem of the funny-looking cabbage-family vegetable kohlrabi is the part you eat. It swells up like a bulb and is crunchy and juicy. It's originally from eastern Europe and tastes like a mild turnip, but it isn't a root vegetable. You can cook kohlrabi as you'd cook potatoes or turnips, though it's also good raw—you can use grated kohlrabi in salads or slaws. As part of the cabbage family, kohlrabi is another highly nutritious vegetable that's easy to grow in spring and fall in the Mid-Atlantic.

The swollen stem of the kohlrabi plant is what we eat.

## ■ *Recommended Varieties*

'Express Forcer', 'Winner', 'Kolibri', and 'Rapid Star' are recommended varieties to plant.

## ■ *When and Where to Plant*

**Temperature:** Kohlrabi needs a minimum soil temperature of 55°F to germinate. It is the least frost hardy of all cabbage-family plants, so plan fall plantings so that it can mature before nighttime temperatures are routinely in the 40sF. In the Coastal Plain and Piedmont sow seeds outside from mid-August through mid-September for a fall harvest. In the Mountains and Plateau, sow seeds outside in July for a fall harvest. Plant transplants outside in April and May for spring/summer harvests in all areas.

**Soil:** Plants thrive in soil with a pH of 6.0 to 6.5. Add compost to the soil before planting.

**Sun:** Full sun, especially during cooler weather.

## ▉ *How to Plant*

**Starting seeds indoors:** You can start seeds indoors a month before you want to plant them outside. However, it is just as easy to grow kohlrabi from seeds sown directly into the garden.

**Planting outside:** Plant outside, leaving 8 to 12 inches between transplants and 3 to 4 inches between seeds. (You can thin the plants after they germinate. The "baby kohlrabi" plants are good in stir fries.)

## ▉ *How to Grow*

**Water:** Keep seeds and seedlings moist while germinating; then monitor and keep evenly moist throughout the growing season.

**Fertilizer:** Kohlrabi is not a heavy feeder but will benefit from sidedressing with a balanced fertilizer midway through the growing season.

**Pest control:** Kohlrabi is more resistant to pests than some cabbage family members, but it still has problems sometimes with flea beetles and cabbageworms. You can use Neem oil to control flea beetles. Floating row covers can prevent flea beetle damage and damage from cabbage-worms. If you see worms, spray with *Bacillus thuringiensis* (*B.t.*).

## ▉ *When and How to Harvest*

Harvest kohlrabi by pulling up the entire plant. Start harvesting when the stems are 1 inch in diameter, and continue to harvest until the stems are 3 inches in diameter. If you let the stems grow any larger, the vegetables will be woody, fibrous, and tough. This is a vegetable that can confuse gardeners, because the vegetables you buy at the grocery store are sometimes much larger than what you'll harvest at home. Don't be tempted to let your kohlrabi grow too long to match your idea of what it's supposed to look like.

---

**GROWING TIPS**

Plant kohlrabi seeds every three weeks during the planting season to enjoy successive harvests. Most varieties mature within 40 to 50 days, so planting frequently will allow you to harvest a fresh crop for several months.

If you are sowing seeds in summer for a fall harvest, provide the seedlings with some shade to protect them from the scorching sun.

Use a blanket or sheet to protect plants from cold weather, including late-spring and early-fall frosts. Temperatures in the 40sF after the plants have been growing a while can cause the plants to bolt and flower, resulting in a loss of the crop.

# LEEK *(Allium ampeloprasum,* Porrum Group*)*

I love leeks. They're so easy to grow, and they're fun to cook with. You can throw young, tender leeks on the grill. Or you can cut up larger leeks to make potato and leek soup. (Sauté 8 cups of chopped-up leeks until soft. Add 8 cups of diced potatoes and cover with chicken broth. Simmer until the potatoes are tender. Purée the vegetables. Pour in 1 cup of heavy cream. Delicious!) One thing to be careful about when cooking with leeks: because you blanch the stems by hilling the leeks (see Growing Tip), a lot of soil and grit can get stuck between the leaves. I always cut them in half lengthwise and spend quality time washing them before chopping them up. Then I wash them again after chopping, tossing them in a colander to get any remaining grit out.

## ■ Recommended Varieties

'Lancelot' is a good variety to plant in for a fall and winter harvest. It is one of the most cold-tolerant types. 'Leefall' is very cold-hardy and will overwinter in all but the coldest areas of the Mid-Atlantic. Grow 'Jolant' and 'Dawn Giant' through the summer for summer and early fall harvests.

## ■ When and Where to Plant

**Temperature:** Leeks take a long time to mature, and they require cool temperatures to grow. In the Coastal Plain areas, it's best to plant leeks from seed in fall and let them grow throughout the winter. You can also plant transplants of warmer-weather varieties in March to grow through the summer. Plant transplants in all other areas in March and let them mature throughout the summer.

**Soil:** Add compost to the soil before planting. Leeks grow best in loose soils full of organic matter. Test the soil to ensure a pH of 6.5 to 7.0.

**Sun:** Full sun.

---

### GROWING TIPS

To get long, white stems, you have to hill leeks. As the plants grow, pile the soil up around the bottom leaves—just to the bottom of the leaf fork. This will encourage the plant to keep growing upward and forming new leaves at the top of the plant.

An alternative method in well-drained soils is to plant leeks in a shallow trench (4 to 6 inches deep). As the leeks grow, fill in the trench.

Keep the leek patch weeded. The one thing leeks are picky about is weeds.

## ▪ *How to Plant*

**Starting seeds indoors:** Start seeds indoors eight to ten weeks before you plan to plant leeks outdoors. You can sow eight to ten seeds per 4-inch pot and then tease apart the roots when you're ready to plant outside.

**Planting outside:** Sow seeds 2 inches apart outside and thin to 6 inches after plants have two sets of leaves. When planting transplants, harden off before planting in the garden. Leave 4 to 6 inches between plants when transplanting in the garden.

## ▪ *How to Grow*

**Water:** For the best flavor, keep leeks evenly moist throughout the growing season. Do not let them dry out.

**Fertilizer:** Leeks are not heavy feeders. Sidedress with a balanced fertilizer every two months during the growing season.

**Pest control:** Leeks are fairly pest free.

Both the white root and the green leaves of the leeks can be eaten.

## ▪ *When and How to Harvest*

Leeks mature in 100 to 120 days, depending on the variety. Once the stalks reach ½ inch in diameter, you can start harvesting them, though. If you've planted a lot of leeks (a 4-square-foot patch, for example), you'll have plenty of plants to harvest over a period of time. You can pull the younger plants to use in salads, omelets, and other quick-cook meals and save some plants to grow larger for use in soups and stocks. Harvest leeks by pulling up the entire plant.

Most people cook with the tender, mild white part of the leeks. You can use the green tops for flavoring broth and soups, too.

# LETTUCE *(Lactuca sativa)*

Lettuce is the quintessential cool-season crop. It isn't just the cool weather that lettuce likes, though. Lettuce needs the short days (and long nights) associated with fall, winter, and early spring to stay in a vegetative state—producing leaves not flowers. Once the weather starts to heat up, lettuce leaves get tough and bitter, and plants will send up a flower stalk. Pollinators of your summer vegetables love lettuce flowers, so once you're done harvesting for leaves, let some of the plants flower to draw these beneficial insects to your garden. Once you start growing your own lettuce, you'll be amazed at the amount of money you can save. Buying fresh looseleaf lettuce at the market is expensive!

## ■ Recommended Varieties

There are four types of lettuce: crisphead, butterhead, romaine, and looseleaf. Butterhead and looseleaf are the easiest types to grow in the Mid-Atlantic. Romaine and crisphead don't do well in our heat. 'Black-Seeded Simpson' and 'Simpson Elite' are two good green-leaf varieties. 'Red Sails' and 'Lolla Rosa' are easy-to-grow red-leaf varieties. Try 'Buttercrunch' if you want a heading lettuce. You can find a variety of mesclun and cut-and-come-again seed mixes at garden centers and home-improvement stores—all of these will do fine if grown in fall or spring in the Mid-Atlantic.

## ■ When and Where to Plant

**Temperature:** Lettuce is a short-day, cool-season crop. For a fall planting, sow seeds outside from August 1 through September 15 in all regions. Sow outdoors from December 15 to March 15 for winter and spring harvesting in the Coastal Plain. Sow outdoors in late March through late April in the Piedmont and in April and May in the Mountain and Plateau areas.

**Soil:** Lettuce needs a soil pH of 6.0 to 7.0. Because it is a heavy feeder, you can save yourself work by adding compost to the soil before planting.

**Sun:** Full to partial sun; sometimes lettuces will last longer into the summer if planted in partial shade.

Use scissors to snip off lettuce leaves, and they will grow back.

**GROWING TIPS**

Cover lettuce seeds planted outside with seed-starting mix rather than garden soil. It is hard for tender lettuce seedlings to break through a hard soil crust.

Sow some lettuce seeds around summer plants such as tomatoes and peppers. You can get a second late-spring crop of lettuce this way.

Lettuce is shallow rooted, so be careful when harvesting. It's better to cut leaf lettuce than to pull or twist off leaves. You don't want to yank the whole plant out of the ground.

## How to Plant

**Starting seeds indoors:** You can start lettuce seeds indoors, but it's so easy to grow lettuce from seed outdoors that it really isn't worth the time or hassle to start indoors.

**Planting outside:** Sow seeds outdoors and cover with seed-starting mix. Press the soil down and water. (Pressing the soil cover down helps keep the seeds from floating away.) Sow head lettuce seeds with 1 inch between seeds. Thin to 4 inches after the plants have three sets of leaves. Thin to 12-inch spacing as the plants start to mature. Eat what you thin! Sow cut-and-come-again lettuces and leaf lettuces thickly—three seeds per inch.

## How to Grow

**Water:** Keep the soil evenly moist.

**Fertilizer:** Lettuce likes to eat. As with all leaf crops, lettuce responds well to applications of composted chicken manure.

**Pest control:** Slugs are a major problem with lettuce. Spread diatomaceous earth around lettuce plants to create a barrier for slugs.

## When and How to Harvest

Harvest head lettuce by pulling up the entire plant. Harvest leaf lettuce by using scissors to snip off leaves about ½ to 1 inch above the soil line. The leaf lettuce will grow back. Always harvest in the morning when the water content of the leaves is highest. I like to use a salad spinner to wash homegrown lettuce. Fill the bowl with cold water and swish the leaves around. Dump them out into the strainer to drain. Repeat. Then spin the water away from the leaves, drain the bowl, and keep the lettuce in the salad spinner in the refrigerator. The lettuce will remain crunchy and crisp.

# ONION *(Allium cepa)*

For best results, grow short-day onions in the Mid-Atlantic.

You almost can't cook without onions. They're so inexpensive to buy that you might wonder why you should bother growing them. The reason to consider growing onions is that if you select the right varieties, they're fairly easy to grow throughout the winter and require little care. You can grow onions from seeds, bulbs (also called sets), and transplants. There are short-, long-, and intermediate-day onions. Your local garden center should carry onion types that are right for your area. Bunching onions, also called green onions, never form bulbs and can grow anywhere.

## ■ Recommended Varieties

**Bunching types:** 'White Sweet Spanish', 'Long White Summer Bunching' (will often survive the winter), 'Deep Purple', 'Feast'.

**Plants (bulbing):** 'Mars', 'Giant Red Hamburger', 'Super Star', 'Candy', 'Prince', 'Copra', 'Alisa Craig', 'Sweet Sandwich', 'Walla Walla'.

**Sets (bulbing):** These varieties are good for storage. 'Ebenezer', 'Southport Red Globe', 'Stuttgart' type.

## GROWING TIPS

Make sure you are purchasing varieties with proven track records in your area.

Mulch onions to keep weeds down, the soil temperature cool, and moisture levels even. Eat the immature bulbing onions that you pull up during thinning as you would eat green onions.

Don't add sulfur to the soil where you're growing onions—it will cause the onions to have an off taste.

## ■ *When and Where to Plant*

**Temperature:** Plant onions outside April 1–15 in the Mountain and Plateau areas, and in March in the Piedmont and Coastal Plain. Plant bunching onions outside in September for fall harvests.

**Soil:** Onions grow best in loamy soils. You'll have to fertilize more if you are growing onions in sandy soil. Clay soils produce more pungent onions.

**Sun:** Full sun.

## ■ *How to Plant*

**Starting seeds indoors:** Start onion seeds indoors six weeks before you plan to transplant them outdoors.

**Planting outside:** If planting seeds, you can sow up to four weeks earlier than if you are planting transplants. Plant bunching onions close together (2 inches apart) and bulbing onions 6 inches apart.

## ■ *How to Grow*

**Water:** Onions don't require a lot of water, but they do need even moisture. Dry soil will cause the onion to produce two bulbs instead of one. Increase watering as the bulb begins to form and swell. Decrease watering in the last two weeks before harvesting.

**Fertilizer:** Incorporate a balanced, slow-release fertilizer into the planting bed before planting onions. If you are growing onions in sandy soil, sidedress every four weeks during the growing season only. Avoid high-nitrogen fertilizer because it can cause onions to be less winter hardy and produce smaller bulbs.

**Pest control:** Onion root maggots are the most problematic pests for onions. Good sanitation, to remove dead plant leaves, will help control onion maggots.

## ■ *When and How to Harvest*

Harvest bunching onions when they grow to be at least ⅓ inch in diameter. Pull up the entire plant, and chop it up for use in salads, soups, stews, and sandwiches.

Bulbing onions have a more delicate harvesting process. A month before you want to harvest the onions, start gradually pulling the soil away from the bulbs. By harvest time, the bulbs should be one-third uncovered. Pull up the onions when one-third of the tops have fallen over. Lay them on top of the soil and allow them to cure (dry out) for three to five days. Cover the plants if rain is forecast. Before bringing the onions inside, cut the tops off, leaving 1 inch of stalk to dry on the plants. You can store short-day onions for two to three months in a cool environment with low humidity.

# PARSNIP *(Pastinaca sativa)*

Parsnips are relatives of carrots, but they're sweeter with a buttery, smooth flavor. You don't want to eat parsnips raw, but they taste great cooked, either roasted or in soups and stews. These cold-hardy vegetables require many of the same growing conditions as carrots. They're high in vitamin C, fiber, and folate, and they're easy to grow once they germinate. Put these in your "plant and forget" category of vegetables.

## Recommended Varieties

There aren't a lot of varieties of parsnips. Grow what you can find.

## When and Where to Plant

**Temperature:** Plant parsnips in the Mountain and Plateau areas outside from April 1–May 1. Plant parsnips outside in September to grow through the winter in the Coastal Plain and Piedmont regions.

**Soil:** Parsnips need a pH of 6.0 to 6.5 and deep, workable, loose soil. Hard clay soils can cause forked roots. Dig compost into the planting bed before planting.

**Sun:** Plant in full sun to partial shade.

Like carrots, parsnips need deep, loose soil to grow well.

**GROWING TIPS**

Buy seeds packed for your growing year. Parsnip seeds have a short shelf life.

Parsnips can take a while to germinate. Make sure the bed where you planted the seeds stays consistently moist while you're waiting for the plants to sprout.

Parsnip leaves can cause a skin rash in some people. Always wear long sleeves and gloves when handling the plants.

## How to Plant

**Starting seeds indoors:** Not recommended.

**Planting outside:** Soak seeds for 24 hours before planting. Sow seeds thickly outside—at a rate of three or four seeds per inch. Cover with seed-starting mix, and water. You might want to cover with frost cloth to help keep the soil from drying out during germination. Parsnips take up to 20 days to germinate, and the soil can't completely dry out during that time. Thin seedlings to 4 inches apart once they germinate and have two sets of leaves.

## How to Grow

**Water:** Keep the soil evenly moist, and water deeply so that the top 6 inches of soil are soaked when you water.

**Fertilizer:** Sidedress with a balanced fertilizer once a month during the growing season.

**Pest control:** Parsnips are fairly pest free. If rabbits and squirrels are a problem in your area, use a floating row cover for young plants. Black swallowtail caterpillars will sometimes feast on the plant leaves. You can pick these off by hand or wait for them to go away. They won't stay all fall.

## When and How to Harvest

Parsnips are ready to harvest when the root tops are 1½ to 2 inches in diameter. Use a garden fork to loosen the soil around the parsnips and help dig them up. It takes 120 to 150 days for parsnips to grow from seed to maturity, and by that time they're well rooted in. Parsnips always taste better when they've been exposed to cool weather.

Growing your own peas can save you money at the grocery store.

# PEA *(Pisum sativum)*

Everyone can grow peas. They are, hands down, the easiest vegetable to grow. You can grow shelling peas (that you remove from the shell before eating) and edible-podded peas (such as snap or snow peas). Pea shoots, the top 6 inches of growth on the pea plant, are also edible. Cook pea shoots like you'd cook braising greens, or sauté them in olive oil and lemon juice with a bit of garlic, and toss with pasta. Yum! Peas are another vegetable that will save you a lot of money if you grow your own. It's expensive to buy tasty fresh peas but inexpensive to grow them.

If you want to pick delicious peas and eat them right out of the garden, grow sugar snap or snow peas. Recommended varieties are 'Sugar Snap', 'Mammoth Melting Sugar', 'Snowbird', and 'Sugar Bon'. Try these varieties of shelling peas: 'Wando', 'Green Arrow', 'Freezonian', and 'Tall Telephone'.

## ■ *When and Where to Plant*

**Temperature:** If you plant two successive groups of peas, they'll ripen at different times so that you're not overwhelmed with more peas than you know what to do with. In the Coastal Plain and Piedmont, plant peas outside from mid-February through mid-March. Plant peas in the Plateau and Mountain regions in mid-March through early April.

**Soil:** Peas do not need excellent soil. As legumes, they fix their own nitrogen—in effect making their own food.

**Sun:** Full sun.

## ◼ *How to Plant*

**Starting seeds indoors:** Not recommended.

**Planting outside:** Use a hoe to dig rows 1 inch deep (even in raised beds). Plant rows 8 inches apart in raised beds and 18 inches apart in regular garden beds. Space seeds 2 inches apart when planting.

## ◼ *How to Grow*

**Water:** Keep the soil evenly moist but not soaking wet. Do not allow the bed to completely dry out.

**Fertilizer:** Do not over fertilize peas with nitrogen. Too much nitrogen can cause lots of green growth and no flowers. No flowers equals no peas! If you have poor soil, sidedress with a lower nitrogen fertilizer when plants are 6 inches tall. The phosphorus and potassium will encourage good fruit development, and that's what you want to eat—the fruits!

**Pest control:** Aphids are the biggest pest problem for peas. Use insecticidal soap according to package instructions to control the pests.

## ◼ *When and How to Harvest*

Pick or clip off individual pea pods to harvest. Peas will be ready for harvest about 60 days after planting.

Harvest snap peas when the pods are plum but still dark green in color. Harvest snow peas when the pods are still relatively flat. The flowers might still be hanging on to the ends of the pods of both types of peas when you harvest the pods.

Harvest shelling peas when the pods are plump but still dark green. Once the pods start to turn yellow, the sugars in the peas convert to starch and they aren't tasty anymore.

---

### GROWING TIPS

Place pea stakes or supports as soon as you see the plants germinating. They grow fast, and it's nearly impossible to wrestle a staking system into place once the plants are taller than 6 inches.

If you have poor germination rates, the peas could have succumbed to a fungal problem. Try again with a different variety that's disease resistant.

If you have tall plants but few peas, pinch off the growing tip of the plant to encourage more fruit production.

# RADISH *(Raphanus sativus)*

Radishes are cool-season root vegetables. The roots are the most commonly eaten part of the radish, but the tops are edible, too. Spring radishes are fast to germinate and mature. You can get several radish crops from one package of seeds. Radishes are beneficial plants for the vegetable garden, too, because they deter pests and, when allowed to flower, attract beneficial insects and pollinators. It's a good idea to sow successive crops of radishes so that they mature a few weeks apart. Nobody needs sixty radishes at once!

## ■ *Recommended Varieties*

You can find infinite varieties of radishes in the store. 'Cherry Belle' is the typical round, red-on-the-outside, white-on-the-inside variety that most people think of when they think "radish." 'French Breakfast' radishes have longer roots. You can also purchase seed mixes with red, white, purple, and yellow radishes in them.

Because radishes grow so quickly, they are a good plant for children to grow.

**GROWING TIPS**

Plant successive crops of radishes so that they don't mature all at once.

Let some radishes stay in the garden to flower. This will attract beneficial insects and pollinators to your summer crops.

## When and Where to Plant

**Temperature:** The soil temperature has to be at least 50°F for radishes to germinate. In the Coastal Plain and Piedmont, plant radishes outside from late March through May. In the Mountains plant radishes outside in April and May.

**Soil:** Radishes are not picky about soil, but, as root crops, they will rot if the soil is slow draining or wet.

**Sun:** Full sun.

## How to Plant

**Starting seeds indoors:** Not recommended.

**Planting outside:** Sow successive plantings of radish seeds outside as soon as the soil can be worked and has drained. Plant seeds ½ inch deep and 2 inches apart. Radishes have a high germination rate. The more space you put between the seeds, the less thinning you'll have to do.

## How to Grow

**Water:** Radishes aren't fussy, but they do need even moisture levels to avoid cracking.

**Fertilizer:** To grow larger roots, you can fertilize with fish emulsion two weeks after planting.

**Pest control:** Use row covers to prevent flea beetles and aphids from attacking the plants. You can also spray with insecticidal soap. For the most part, though, radishes are so fast-growing, it's not worth the trouble to try to control any pests on them.

## When and How to Harvest

Don't let the radishes linger. They taste best when harvested after three to four weeks of growth, whey they are still relatively small. The older the radishes, the more fibrous and stringy they get, and the more pungent the flavor becomes.

# SPINACH *(Spinaceia oleracea)*

Why should you grow your own spinach? Because field-grown and harvested spinach is easily contaminated, and, if you like to eat your spinach raw, that can cause unpleasant intestinal problems. Spinach is a cool-season green grown for its leaves. You can actually overwinter spinach, even in the mountains, if it is planted with enough time to grow to some size before winter. Spinach is a long-day flowering plant, which means it stays vegetative during the short days of fall, winter, and spring. As soon as the temperature starts to warm up and the days lengthen, spinach will start to bolt, or flower, and the season's over.

## ■ Recommended Varieties

Plant different varieties of spinach in the spring and fall.

**Fall:** 'Space' (semi-savoy), 'Tyee' (semi-savoy).
**Spring:** 'Melody' (savoy), 'UniPack 151' (savoy), 'Nordic IV' (smooth leaf), 'Olympia' (smooth leaf).

## ■ When and Where to Plant

**Temperature:** Spinach will germinate in soil temperatures of 45°F to 75°F. It grows best with air temperatures of 60°F to 65°F. Plant seeds or transplants outside in April and May in the Plateau and Mountain regions, and in March and April in the Coastal Plain and Piedmont regions. The soil needs to be workable in order to plant spinach. Sow

---

**GROWING TIPS**

Sow successive plantings to ensure fresh harvests of tender young leaves over a longer period of time.

Use drip irrigation or soaker hoses to provide steady water at the root zone and away from the leaves. Fungal diseases that plague spinach can spread through water on the leaves.

Once spinach sends up a flower stalk, pull up the plant, and compost it. There's no use in trying to keep the plant in a vegetative state once it has moved on.

Spinach is partially hardy but can be affected by frosts. If temperatures are forecast to be below 28°F, cover with frost cloth. Don't pull up your spinach in the winter, though. Even if you get snow, it might just pull through and get a head start on spring.

seeds again outside in August for fall harvests in all areas.

**Soil:** Spinach needs a soil with a pH of 6.0 to 7.5. It is a leaf crop and as such is a heavy feeder. Add compost to the soil before planting to ensure healthy growth.

**Sun:** Full sun.

## ◼ *How to Plant*

**Starting seeds indoors:** Start seeds indoors a month before you want to transplant outdoors. Working with transplants is easier for spring crops than for fall crops.

**Planting outside:** Soak seeds overnight before planting outside. Sow fall crops directly outside into the garden to avoid problems with bolting. Space seeds 2 inches apart and thin to 6 inches apart after plants have three sets of leaves. Harden off transplants and plant 6 inches apart.

With a little planning, you can overwinter spinach anywhere in the Mid-Atlantic.

## ◼ *How to Grow*

**Water:** Spinach is not a heavy drinker, but keep the soil evenly moist, and avoid wet/dry/wet/dry situations.

**Fertilizer:** Spinach is a leaf crop and a heavy feeder. Sidedress with a balanced fertilizer every two weeks during the growing season.

**Pest control:** Prevent fungal problems by keeping water off the leaves. Use floating row covers to prevent damage from leaf miners.

## ◼ *When and How to Harvest*

You can start harvesting spinach leaves three weeks after planting or when the plants have at least ten leaves on them. Cut the outermost leaves first, always leaving six leaves on the plant to produce sugars to help the plant keep growing. Use scissors or pinch off the leaves at the base of the leaf stalk. Spinach matures in about 40 days. You can also wait until that point and harvest the entire plant.

# SWISS CHARD *(Beta vulgaris chicla)*

Swiss chard is a biennial green related to beets. Both the colorful leaves and the stalks of the plants are edible. It will grow through the summer if planted during cool weather, making it one of those hard-to-define vegetables, in terms of seasons. Swiss chard is loaded with vitamins and is multipurpose in the kitchen. Young leaves can be picked and added raw to salad. Larger leaves can be added to soups and stews, omelets, sandwiches, and stir-fries. Swiss chard is so pretty that it doesn't have to be contained in the vegetable garden. If you're short on space, grow this beautiful vegetable in the perennial flower garden. It will look right at home.

## ■ *Recommended Varieties*

'Bright Lights' is a multicolored mixture of plants with stems ranging from yellow to white to red to green. 'Rainbow' is another multicolored mix. 'Fordhook Giant' produces large green leaves with white stems.

Swiss chard is pretty enough to grow in a flower garden.

## ■ *When and Where to Plant*

**Temperature:** Swiss chard grows best in cool temperatures. Plant outside in May in the Plateau and Mountain regions. Plant outside in March and April and again in September or October in the Piedmont and Coastal Plain regions.

**Soil:** Swiss chard is not a picky plant and will grow in almost any soil. Add compost before planting, if possible.

**Sun:** Full sun to partial shade.

## ■ *How to Plant*

**Starting seeds indoors:** Not necessary.

**Planting outside:** If you plant transplants purchased from the garden center, space plants at least 8 inches apart. Swiss chard grows to be fairly large. To sow seeds directly out into the garden, soak seeds overnight before planting. Plant one seed every 2 inches, ½ inch deep.

## ■ *How to Grow*

**Water:** Keep chard evenly moist.

**Fertilizer:** Fertilize with a balanced fertilizer every two to four weeks during the growing season.

**Pest control:** Use insecticidal soap to take care of any aphids or leaf miners that might attack.

## ■ *When and How to Harvest*

You can start harvesting Swiss chard leaves as soon as the plant has at least four or five leaves. Take the outermost leaves first, and allow the inner leaves to grow and provide sugars for the pant. Use a sharp knife, scissors, or hand pruners to cut the leaf stalks at the soil level.

---

**GROWING TIPS**

Thin plants once they are 3 or 4 inches tall so that there's one plant every 6 inches.

Leave Swiss chard in the garden throughout the summer, taking care to give it extra water. This is one green that you can grow virtually year-round in most areas of the Mid-Atlantic.

# TURNIP *(Brassica rapa* spp. *rapa)*

Turnips are double-duty plants. You can eat the tops (greens) and the roots. They're a cool-weather vegetable that grows well in early spring in the Mid-Atlantic. If you time it right, you can get a fall crop out of the garden, too. When you think of a turnip, you probably think of large, purple or white, globe-shaped roots, but there are other smaller, sweeter varieties, too. If you've never thought much about turnips, give them a try. They're naturally high in vitamin C and easy to grow.

## ■ *Recommended Varieties*

Traditional large turnip varieties include 'Purple Top', 'White Globe', and 'White Lady'. The 'All Top' variety is grown specifically for turnip greens. 'Hakurei' is a small, white salad turnip that tastes good when shredded raw into salads.

## ■ *When and Where to Plant*

**Temperature:** Turnips will sprout when the weather is warm, but they need cool temperatures to mature if you want to harvest larger roots than

Turnips are grown both for their leafy green tops and their bulbous roots.

**GROWING TIPS**

Plant turnips every three weeks during the optimum planting time for a staggered harvest.

Thin turnips to 4-inch spacing when the plants are 4 inches tall. You can eat the young greens that you pull up. Harvest every other plant when the roots are 1 inch in diameter. This will give you fresh turnips to eat immediately while allowing room for half of the harvest to grow larger roots.

tops. Sow seeds directly into the garden from August 1 to October 1 and again in March and April in the Coastal Plain and Piedmont regions. Sow outside in late April and early May in the Mountain and Plateau areas.

**Soil:** The biggest concern with turnips is to avoid planting them in exactly the same place that you grew cabbage and cabbage-family plants.

**Sun:** Full sun.

## ■ *How to Plant*

**Starting seeds indoors:** Not recommended.

**Planting outside:** Sow turnip seeds thinly (two seeds per inch) outside and cover with seed-starting mix. Turnips germinate quickly and will sprout within a few days. They also have a very high germination rate. If you plant a lot of seeds in a small area, expect to spend time thinning.

## ■ *How to Grow*

**Water:** Keep the soil evenly moist but not soggy.

**Fertilizer:** Add compost to the bed before planting and you won't have to add additional fertilizer. If you have sandy soil, fertilize once with a balanced fertilizer about three weeks after planting.

**Pest control:** Aphids can be controlled with insecticidal soap. Control flea beetles by using row covers.

## ■ *When and How to Harvest*

How you harvest depends on which part of the plant you want to harvest. Young, tender greens can be picked for salads when they are 2 to 4 inches tall. Pull up the young, tender roots when they are 2 inches in diameter, and use them raw in salads. When the larger roots grow to 3 or 4 inches in diameter, they're ready to be pulled up and used for roasting and mashing. The greens can be braised or added to soups. Turnips have a sweeter flavor when allowed to mature when the weather is cooler.

Cool-season herbs cut for use as garnishes.

# *Cool-Season Herbs*

Many of our favorite herbs grow best when the weather is cool. Dill, fennel, and cilantro are just a few of the everyday herbs we use that thrive during the early spring. Some of these herbs will hang on and grow in summer if provided with protection from the sun while others just physiologically won't stay vegetative once the days get longer—their fragrant leaves give way to flowers and seeds. Don't miss out on your favorite seasonings. Plant the herbs covered in this section during the cool-weather growing season.

Parsley

# CILANTRO/CORIANDER
## *(Coriandrum sativum)*

Cilantro is an annual cool-season herb prized for its fragrant leaves. Either you love cilantro or you hate it. I love it. This parsley-family plant grows best in the Mid-Atlantic in spring and early summer. Once the days get longer and hotter, it bolts, sending up a flower stalk that produces seeds. Cilantro seeds are the herb that we call coriander. Don't frustrate yourself growing this herb when the weather is warm. Plant it in spring, and learn how to enjoy it with hearty cool-weather fare.

We use the leaves of cilantro in salsas, but they are also tasty in salads and curries.

# When and Where to Plant

**Temperature:** Cilantro grows best in temperatures of 50°F to 85°F. Sow seeds outside in February and March in the Coastal Plain, in March through May in the Piedmont, and in April and May in the Mountain and Plateau areas. You can "winter sow" this herb by throwing seed out into the vegetable bed at any point in the winter. When the weather is warm enough for it to sprout, it will.

**Soil:** The herb grows well in soils that are slightly alkaline, with a pH of 7.0 or above.

**Sun:** Full sun to partial shade; planting in partial shade will extend the harvest window slightly.

# How to Plant

**Starting seeds indoors:** Not recommended.

**Planting outside:** Plant seeds ¼ inch deep, with two seeds per inch.

# How to Grow

**Water:** Keep seeds moist while sprouting, and avoid wet/dry/wet/dry periods while growing.

**Fertilizer:** Fertilize with a balanced fertilizer two weeks after germination.

**Pest control:** Cilantro has few pest problems but is susceptible to some fungal diseases spread through splashing water. Try to water the plants at the root zone and avoid splashing the water.

# When and How to Harvest

To harvest leaves, snip the top off the plant. The smallest, most immature leaves have the best flavor. If you want to save coriander seeds, pull up the whole plant once seeds have formed and the plant has turned yellow. Hang it upside down to dry over newspaper to collect the seeds.

---

**GROWING TIP**

Stay on top of weeds while plants are germinating. Because the seeds are slow to germinate, if you let the weeds get out of control, the plants will have a hard time growing. The weeds will outcompete them for water and sun.

Dill leaves can be used in salads, and the seeds in flavoring.

# DILL *(Anethum graveolens)*

I love to pick dill at the same time I'm harvesting salad greens. I wash and keep the dill in the same salad spinner as the lettuce. Then I have herb-flavored salad mix for none of the cost of buying it at the grocery store. Dill is an important addition to the vegetable garden, as it serves as a host plant for native butterfly caterpillars, and its flowers are a nectar source for beneficial insects and pollinators.

## ■ *When and Where to Plant*

**Temperature:** Seeds will germinate with soil temperatures of 50°F to 70°F. While the plant likes to grow during cool weather, it is frost sensitive. Plant dill seeds immediately after danger of frost has passed.

**Soil:** Like its relative the carrot, dill needs well-drained, loose soil.

**Sun:** Full sun.

## ■ *How to Plant*

**Starting seeds indoors:** Not recommended. Dill has a taproot, which makes it difficult to transplant.

**Planting outside:** Sow seeds thickly—two seeds per inch—and cover with seed-starting mix. The seeds can take up to two weeks to germinate. Keep the seeds moist while you look for growth.

## ■ *How to Grow*

**Water:** Keep dill evenly moist.

**Fertilizer:** No extra fertilizer is needed.

**Pest control:** Dill is susceptible to the same pests that eat carrots and parsnips. Keep an eye out for aphids and flea beetles.

## ■ *When and How to Harvest*

The leaves are most fragrant and delicious before the plants start to flower. Use kitchen scissors to snip off leaves. If you want to harvest seeds, allow the plant to flower. As the seeds are forming, keep a close eye on the plants. Pull up the plants and hang them upside down to dry over newspaper to collect the seeds.

### GROWING TIPS

Dill gets pretty tall. Stake larger stems to prevent them from falling over in heavy winds or rains.

Don't be alarmed if you see caterpillars on the plants. The native black swallowtail butterfly loves dill and will munch some of your plants to the ground. If you plant dill in several locations in the garden, you might outsmart the caterpillars and have one stand of dill left unscathed.

For a steady supply of fresh, young leaves, sow several successive plantings of dill throughout early spring.

A black swallowtail caterpillar munching on dill.

# FENNEL *(Foeniculum vulgare* var. *azoricum* and *Foeniculum vulgare* var. *dulce)*

There are two types of fennel: Florence fennel, which is a bulb-forming fennel, and bronze fennel, which is grown primarily for its fragrant and attractive leaves. You can grow bronze fennel all winter long in the warmer regions of the Mid-Atlantic. Florence fennel is a spring-planted, summer-growing, fall-harvested plant that does best in container gardens or raised beds in the Mid-Atlantic.

## ■ *When and Where to Plant*

**Temperature:** Sow seeds outside when the soil temperature is at least 60°F.
**Soil:** Fennel needs well-drained, nutrient-rich soil with a pH of 5.5 to 7.0
**Sun:** Full sun to partial shade; bronze fennel will grow well through the summer if grown in full shade.

## ■ *How to Plant*

**Starting seeds indoors:** Not recommended; fennel has a taproot, which makes it difficult to transplant. If you need to start seeds indoors (in the mountains), plant them in a peat or coir pot that can be planted directly outside without disturbing the plant roots.
**Planting outside:** Sow seeds outdoors, 4 inches apart, and barely cover with seed-starting mix. Thin seeds to 8 inches apart when plants are 4 inches tall. Use the plants you pull up to flavor salads.

## ■ *How to Grow*

**Water:** Fennel is a low-water plant, but you'll need to water it if it doesn't rain at least once a week.
**Fertilizer:** No extra fertilizer is needed.
**Pest control:** Fennel is fairly pest free, but black swallowtail butterfly larvae enjoy munching on it as much as dill and parsley. Let the caterpillars munch. The plant will grow back.

## ■ *When and How to Harvest*

Harvest leaves from both types of fennel by using scissors to snip them off at the base of the plant or where they meet the stem. To harvest Florence fennel bulbs, wait until the plant begins to bloom. Then cut off the flowers, wait a few days, and pull up the entire plant.

The leaves of bronze fennel are edible.

## GROWING TIPS

When the bulb is 2 inches in diameter, start mounding the soil up around it to blanch it (keep it white).

Mulch around fennel plants to keep the roots cool.

# PARSLEY *(Petroselinum crispum)*

Parsley is a cool-season, biennial herb grown for its leaves, which are high in vitamins and minerals. In all areas of the Mid-Atlantic, parsley will overwinter. It might not produce a lot of new leaves during the very coolest weeks, but it will stay alive, primed and ready to grow. During the second year, parsley produces flowers and seeds, which you can save to plant in fall or the following spring. Parsley is a great addition to cold salads, soups, and sandwiches.

## ▪ *When and Where to Plant*

**Temperature:** Parsley seeds will germinate with soil temperatures of 50°F to 85°F. They grow best in air temperatures of 60°F. You can plant parsley transplants outside from September to November and again from January to March in Coastal Regions. Plant transplants outside in early April in all other areas.

**Soil:** Parsley grows best in soils with a pH of 6.5 to 7.5 that are well draining and high in organic matter.

**Sun:** Full sun to partial shade.

Curly parsley

Flat-leaf Italian parsley

## How to Plant

**Starting seeds indoors:** Start seeds indoors at least one month before you want to transplant outside. Parsley can be tricky to start from seed. Soak seeds for 12 hours before planting.

**Planting outside:** Sow seeds outside at one seed per inch. It can take two to three weeks for parsley seeds to germinate. You can thin the plants to 4-inch spacing once they've germinated.

## How to Grow

**Water:** Parsley won't need extra water unless the area is experiencing a drought.

**Fertilizer:** Parsley is a heavy feeder. Sidedress with a balanced fertilizer every four weeks during the growing season.

**Pest control:** The main pest that you'll see on parsley is actually the larval form of the black swallowtail butterfly. These caterpillars will feed on parsley for a few weeks and then disappear.

## When and How to Harvest

Keep parsley growing by frequently cutting the outermost leaves for use in the kitchen. You can prolong leaf growth by cutting back the flower stalks for a time. Eventually, though, parsley will flower, set seed, and die.

**GROWING TIPS**

If you have trouble growing parsley from seed, you can buy transplants locally. However, unlike some vegetables and herbs, you don't get much choice of varieties if you don't grow your own from seed.

Marigolds serve to ward off pests and attract pollinators in this raised bed garden filled with peppers. Mulch keeps moisture in the soil and helps with weed control.

# *Warm-Season Gardening Tips & Tricks*

The warm-season vegetable gardening season in the Mid-Atlantic runs from May through September in the Coastal Plain and Interior Foothills or Piedmont. It runs from June through August in the Mountain and Plateau areas.

Most of the warm-season vegetables and herbs that we grow are originally from tropical regions. They are tender to frost and don't grow well during cool weather. While they might hang on if temperatures are above freezing but not yet warm, they won't grow.

The biggest mistake that new gardeners make is to plant warm-season vegetables too early. Just because the stores have tomatoes in March doesn't mean you should plant them in March. Unless you're planning to use a cold frame to elevate the temperature, wait to plant the warm-season vegetables until it is actually warm. That means soil temperatures of 60°F to 65°F and nighttime air temperatures of 65°F to 70°F.

## Watering During the Warm Season

Everything during the warm season is expedited, including water use. You might be able to get away with watering your cool-season vegetable garden once or twice a week, but you will frequently need to water every day or every other day during the warm season. The heat causes plants to use more water and causes water to evaporate from the soil more quickly.

Mulching plants can help cut down on watering frequency. When I started mulching my vegetables, I noticed a huge difference. Soaker hoses and drip irrigation are also helpful tools for the warm-season vegetable garden. Many summer vegetables are sensitive to wet/dry/wet/dry conditions. Mulch and a soaker hose can help keep moisture levels steady to avoid problems such as blossom-end rot.

## Planting for Pollination

Cool-season vegetables are primarily just that—the vegetative parts of the plants. Warm-season vegetables are mostly the fruits of the plants, and to get fruits, flowers have to be pollinated. Corn is a wind-pollinated plant, but it is the exception in the vegetable garden, rather than the rule. Most summer vegetables (fruits) are a result of flowers pollinated by insects. You can increase pollination rates by planting flowers in the vegetable garden.

All plants in the aster family attract pollinators. Lettuce and radishes, if you let a few stay in the garden and flower, will attract hundreds of pollinators. Many herbs, if allowed to flower, will also attract beneficial insects and pollinators. Leave space in the warm-season vegetable garden for flowers. It won't be wasted.

## Plants for Pollinators

| | | |
|---|---|---|
| Basil | Mountain mint | Tarragon |
| Bee balm | Purple coneflower | Thyme |
| Lettuce | Radish | Zinnia |
| Marigold | Sunflower | |

## Dealing with Pests

Many more pests are active during the warm season than during the cool season. It can be frustrating at times, dealing with so many pests. You'll see

A row of pollinator plants near the vegetable gardens

that many of the vegetable profiles have recommendations to "use floating row covers" to protect the plants. There are different remedies for pests, listed in the chart beginning on page 67. However, the best two ways to deal with pests have nothing to do with what to spray on the plants.

1. Plant a variety of plants in the garden, and plant groups of the same plant in many places throughout the garden. Diversity is the key to luring beneficial insects and confusing harmful ones. A vegetable garden is not a natural ecosystem, but it can more closely mimic a natural ecosystem if you introduce variety.

2. Raise your threshold for pest damage. I really don't care if pests eat my plants. The one pest that confounds me and drives me to synthetic chemicals is the squash vine borer. I can't grow squash without chemicals because of this pest. Otherwise, I let the pests munch. I find though, that I have few pest problems, because my gardens are so haphazardly planted and include a mishmash of plants all over the place.

Planting a wide variety of vegetables, herbs, and flowers together confuses pests.

# BEAN Bush and Pole Bean *(Phaseolus vulgaris)*
Lima Bean *(Phaseolus lunatus)*

Beans are absolutely warm-weather vegetables. Don't plant these vegetables too early, or you won't get a harvest. There are tons of different varieties of beans, including snap beans—both pole and bush varieties, lima beans, and shelling beans. You can also grow edamame, which are soybeans that you eat while they're still green and tender (but not the pods). Fava beans are the only exception to the warm-weather rule. You plant favas in fall to harvest in spring (in warmer areas) or in early spring for harvest in early summer (in cooler areas). To get a bigger and better bean harvest, inoculate the seeds with nitrogen-fixing bacteria, available online and at natural garden stores.

## ▪ *Recommended Varieties*

What's your goal when growing beans? Ask yourself that before making selections. Do you have space to grow pole beans on trellises, or do you need to grow more compact bush forms? Do you want to harvest lima beans for making your own succotash or fresh snap beans to lightly steam and eat with summer grilled dinners? Here are some good bean selections for the Mid-Atlantic.

### GROWING TIPS

Don't jump the gun with beans. Wait until the soil has warmed to at least 60°F before planting.

Mulch beans with wheat straw, shredded newspaper, and other low-nitrogen materials to keep moisture levels even and weeds to a minimum.

Place supports before the plants grow taller than 3 or 4 inches. It's difficult to get a trellis in place once the beans start growing. You also want pole beans to have something to "grab" as soon as they're tall enough to start climbing.

Grow beans over your sunny trellis in your flower garden. Scarlet runner beans are beautiful ornamentals as well as edibles, and they can be eaten in the pod when young, eaten fresh and shelled when still tender, or eaten as dried beans.

Baby your beans when the weather is hot. Beans will drop flowers and stop producing when temperatures climb above 85°F. If they can hang on until cooler weather arrives, they'll start producing again. If not, you can pull them up and replant so that they mature when the days have cooled off.

Pole beans growing up a trellis

**Snap beans, Bush type:** 'Provider', 'Bush Kentucky Wonder', 'Sequoia', 'Greencrop', 'Derby', 'Royal Burgundy', 'Roma II', 'Jade'.

**Snap beans, pole-type:** 'Emerite', 'Blue Lake', 'Kentucky Blue', 'Kentucky Wonder Green', 'Gold Rush', 'Indy Gold', 'Golden Rod'.

Only purchase snap beans that are resistant to bean common mosaic virus and anthracnose—this will be indicated on the seed packet.

**Lima beans:** You can purchase determinate (which stop growing at a certain height/point in their life cycle) and indeterminate (keep growing indefinitely) lima beans. The indeterminates are usually thought to have better flavor, but they can grow to be huge and need strong trellises for support. Determinate limas grow to heights of 2 feet and can still use some staking—but this is not as crucial as it is for indeterminate types.

## ■ *When and Where to Plant*

**Temperature:** The soil temperature at a 4-inch depth needs to be at least 60°F before planting beans. Planting times will range from late April through early June, depending on where you live. Plant earlier in warmer areas and later in cooler areas. Keep your soil thermometer handy!

**Soil:** Add compost to the soil before planting. Beans will not grow well in soil with a pH below 5.5. Test the pH to ensure it is 6.0 to 7.2.

**Sun:** Full sun; select an area for your pole beans on the north side of the garden so that they won't shade out the rest of your plants as they grow.

## ■ *How to Plant*

**Starting seeds indoors:** Not recommended or needed.

**Planting outside:** Plant beans outside when the soil temperature is at least 60°F at a depth of 1 to 1½ inches. You might have heard the term "a hill of beans." That's because beans are usually seeded in mounds or hills, four or five seeds to a hill. If you plant beans this way, you can then put up a trellis or tomato cage over each hill. If you plant beans to grow along a trellis, plant beans 1 inch deep and 1 inch apart along the bottom of the trellis.

## ■ *How to Grow*

**Water:** Beans are somewhat drought tolerant until they start flowering. Once plants start flowering, the beans should be kept evenly moist.

**Fertilizer:** Beans fix nitrogen, so they do not need high-nitrogen fertilizers. Once beans start flowering, fertilize once with a 0-5-5 or 0-10-10 fertilizer.

**Pest control:** Pest problems include Mexican bean beetles, thrips, aphids, corn earworms, and stinkbugs. Row covers can keep beetles, stinkbugs, and corn earworms away from plants. Use insecticidal soap to control thrips and aphids.

## ■ *When and How to Harvest*

Once pods start forming, it's time to harvest. Snap beans should be picked when the pods are still tender. Beans should be easy to snap off the plant and should easily break in half when they're ready to harvest. Pick in the morning when the plants have the highest moisture content. Beans taste best if eaten soon after harvesting, so pick them on the day you plan to eat them. To keep plants producing, pick regularly. If beans are allowed to yellow on the plant, the plant will stop producing more pods.

To harvest limas and pole types for shelling beans, wait until the pods start bulging and then pick. Pick before the pods turn yellow!

To harvest dry beans, allow the pods to dry on the plant. Then pull up the entire plant and hang it upside down to dry over a clean sheet. You will have to thresh the pods in order to remove the dried bits of pod from the dried beans. (Quite frankly, it's easier and cheaper to just buy dried beans.)

# CORN *(Zea mays)*

Different types of corn include popcorn, sweet corn, and field corn. This section is about sweet corn. Corn is native to North America. It is in the grass family and started out as a wild grass that was gradually domesticated and bred for larger "ears," which hold the seeds. Even if you have a small garden, you can grow corn. You don't have to have an acre. Corn is wind pollinated, so it is more important to plant corn close together in 4 × 4- or 6 × 6-foot blocks than it is to plant a big field.

Corn is a wind-pollinated plant, so you have to plant the plants close together in blocks so the wind can blow the pollen from plant to plant.

## ■ *Recommended Varieties*

**Bicolor:** 'Trinity', 'Temptation', 'Breeder's Bicolor', 'Mystique', 'Providence', 'Serendipity', 'Delectable', 'Seneca Dancer'.

**White:** 'Spring Snow', 'Silver Princess', 'Silverado', 'Avalon', 'Argent'.

**Yellow:** 'Seneca Horizon', 'Early Choice', 'Sundance', 'Sugar Buns', 'Legend', 'Bodacious'.

## ■ *When and Where to Plant*

**Temperature:** Sweet corn does not grow well in cold soil. Wait to plant until soil temperatures are 60°F to 80°F. This period ranges from April through early June in the Mid-Atlantic. The best way to check if it's time to plant corn is to use a soil thermometer.

**Soil:** If you grew peas in spring, plant corn for an early-summer crop. The corn will benefit from the nitrogen fixed by the peas. Before planting, add compost to the soil and work in a balanced, slow-release organic fertilizer.

**Sun:** Full sun.

## ■ *How to Plant*

**Starting seeds indoors:** Not recommended or needed.

**Planting outside:** Wait until the soil has warmed up to plant corn. You can soak seeds in warm water overnight to pre-sprout and ensure germination. If you have space to plant 10 × 10-foot blocks, sow seeds 6 inches apart in rows that are 18 inches apart. If you are growing corn in raised beds, make sure to plant at least twelve stalks spaced 8 inches apart, in a square. You will have to assist with pollination of them by shaking the plants once you see pollen forming.

## ■ *How to Grow*

**Water:** Corn requires consistent moisture through the growing season and more moisture when it starts to flower. If it is drought stressed, the leaves will roll up and the plants will take on a "pointy" appearance.

**Fertilizer:** Corn is a hungry plant. Prepare the planting area by adding compost and a slow-release fertilizer before planting. Fertilize with alfalfa meal and soybean meal when the corn is 2 feet tall and again when it starts to flower.

**Pest control:** There are many pests that attack corn plants. If you've had problems with corn earworm, treat ears with a combination of *B.t.* and mineral oil (1:20) five days after silks emerge. Place five drops on the silks at the end of each ear.

## ■ *When and How to Harvest*

Sweet corn is ready to harvest when the juice that squirts from a kernel pierced by a fingernail is milky white. Start checking the corn after the silks (hairs on the ears) start to turn brown. You can hold the corn stalk in one hand and grasp the ear in the other hand, jerking the ear off the plant without yanking the plant out of the ground.

---

### GROWING TIPS

Corn plants are tall and heavy. To prevent plants from falling over, start to hill up the soil around the base of the plant (to a height of 6 inches) when the plants are 1 foot tall.

Cut off any small plants that sprout from the base of the main stalk. These suckers will sap nutrients from the main plant.

Harvest promptly when the corn is ripe. Overripe corn is tough and chewy.

# CUCUMBER *(Cucumis sativus)*

Cucumbers are warm-season vining vegetables that are part of the squash family. Sometimes you'll hear members of the squash family called "cucurbits." Just as the cabbage family includes many different but related varieties of cold-season vegetables, the cucurbit family includes many related vegetables. This presents somewhat of a challenge, as some of the pests that attack one type of plant in the family can also attack the other types as well. Cucumber beetles, squash vine borers, and several other pests find the summer garden to be an all-you-can-eat buffet of squash-family plants. That's no reason not to grow them, though. Here's how to have success with cucumbers.

## ■ Recommended Varieties

There are several types of cucumbers. Slicers are larger and longer cucumbers made for, you guessed it, slicing. Picklers are shorter, smaller cucumbers. Burpless varieties have thinner skin. There are also vining types and bush types. Bush types are better if you have limited space. Vining types need heavy-duty support in order to produce well. Here are some recommended varieties for the Mid-Atlantic.

**Slicers:** 'Sweet Slice', 'Sweet Success' (AAS), 'Sweet Burpless', 'All Season Burpless', 'Diva'.
**Picklers:** 'Calypso', 'Cool Breeze', 'Patio Pickle', 'Pickalot', 'Salad Bush', 'Orient Express'.

In addition to considering the growth habit of the plant, when shopping for cucumber seeds also look at disease resistance and try to find varieties

with resistance to all or some of the most prevalent cucumber diseases. If you see CMV on the seed packet, it means the cucumber variety is resistant to cucumber mosaic virus. DM means resistance to downy mildew, and PM means resistant to powdery mildew. DM resistance is very important for season long cucumber production.

Growing cucumbers up a trellis saves space in the garden.

# When and Where to Plant

**Temperature:** You can't plant cucumbers until all danger of frost has passed and the soil is at least 60°F. A soil temperature of 70°F is even better. In warmer areas of the Mid-Atlantic, you can plant successive crops for staggered harvesting. Plant seeds outside in late May to early June in the Mountain and Plateau areas. Plant seeds outside in late April to early May in the Coastal Plain and Piedmont regions. (Provided that the soil temperatures are warm enough.)

**Soil:** Cucumbers grow best in soils with a pH of 5.5 to 6.8. They are also heavy feeders and use a lot of water, but they need well-draining soil. Add compost to the soil before planting in order to grow healthy plants.

**Sun:** Full sun.

# How to Plant

**Starting seeds indoors:** Not recommended; cucumbers and other squash plants do not transplant well. They also sprout so quickly that you don't gain anything by starting seeds inside.

**Planting outside:** Sow seeds outside when the soil temperature is at least 60°F and all danger of frost has passed. Allow 8 to 12 inches between plants.

# How to Grow

**Water:** Cucumbers are heavy drinkers. Keep the soil evenly moist during the entire growing period. These plants need more water than almost any other vegetable. Place soaker hoses along the base of cucumber plants to help deliver a steady stream of water at the roots.

**Fertilizer:** Cucumbers need a lot! Sidedress cucumbers every two weeks during the growing season with a balanced fertilizer.

**Pest control:** Cucumber beetles and squash vine borers are the peskiest pests to attack cucumbers. Place floating row covers over young plants, and remove the covers when the plants start flowering. Pyrethrum and Neem oil are two organic pesticides that can help control the pests.

# When and How to Harvest

Once cucumber fruits start forming, keep your eyes peeled for fruits that need to be picked. You can't let cucumbers sit on the vine, because they will start to develop a bitter taste. Fruits left unpicked will also stimulate the plant to stop fruiting. Harvest pickling cucumbers when they are 2 to 6 inches long. Harvest slicing cucumbers when they are 6 to 12 inches long. To see how long the cucumbers you're growing should be at maturity, consult the seed packet. Use pruners to cut the fruits off, leaving 1 inch of stem on the end of the fruit. (This minimizes water loss after harvest.)

# EGGPLANT *(Solanum melongena)*

Eggplants, along with tomatoes, peppers, and tomatillos are members of the nightshade family. If the cucurbit family claims half of the warm-season vegetables we grow, the nightshade family owns the rest. All nightshade vegetables are originally from warmer, tropical locations, and, as such, do not grow well in the cold. At a loss for what to do with eggplants? Two easy ways to eat them are rubbed with olive oil and grilled, and in a ratatouille (summer sauté of tomatoes, squash, and eggplant). If you have the time and patience, make your own eggplant parmesan or lasagna. It will taste so much better than what you can get at a store or restaurant.

## Recommended Varieties

Explore varieties beyond just the "regular" bowling-pin-sized eggplants. There are eggplants that produce long, skinny, dark fruits; light purple fruits; lavender fruits; and white fruits. Here are some varieties to try:

**Regular, large, dark purple type:** 'Black Magic', 'Purple Rain', 'Early Bird'.
**Oriental type (long, skinny fruits):** 'Little Fingers', 'Longtom', 'Ichiban', 'Pintung Long'.
**Other types:** 'Casper' (white fruits), 'Italian Pink Bicolor' (large bell-shaped fruit with pink stripes).

## When and Where to Plant

**Temperature:** Eggplants need soil and nighttime air temperatures to be at least 65°F to grow. You can plant outside in May in the Coastal Plain and Piedmont and in early June in the Plateau and Mountain regions.
**Soil:** The pH should be 6.0 to 6.5 for best growth. Add compost to the soil before planting, and plant in well-drained locations.
**Sun:** Full sun to partial shade; needs full sun in mountains.

## How to Plant

**Starting seeds indoors:** If you want to grow your own transplants, start seeds indoors six to eight weeks before you want to plant outside. Use a heat mat and grow lights for strong plants.
**Planting outside:** Plant transplants outside with 12 to 18 inches between plants. (You can get away with closer spacing in raised beds—12-inch centers (12 inches between plants) work in these.)

## How to Grow

**Water:** Eggplants need a large, consistent supply of water. Use soaker hoses around plants for the best result.

**Fertilizer:** Feed eggplants every two weeks with a balanced fertilizer. They like to eat.

**Pest control:** Many pests and diseases call eggplants home. Colorado potato beetles, tomato hornworms, and flea beetles are the worst insect offenders. Keep plants under row covers until they have three sets of leaves to avoid problems with flea beetles. Keep an eye out for tomato hornworms and handpick them off. (Gross, but effective.) Look for the orange eggs of the Colorado potato beetle on the undersides of the leaves and wash the leaves with water or crush the eggs to control them. *Bacillus thuringiensis* (*B.t.*) is effective on adult beetles.

Eggplants come in different shapes and sizes. Look at your seed packet to tell what they're supposed to look like when ripe so you know when to harvest.

## ■ *When and How to Harvest*

The biggest question with eggplants is, when are they ready to harvest? To know the right answer, you need to pay attention to the seed packet or plant label. Some eggplants grow to be 6 or 8 inches long, while others max out at 4 inches. If you leave the fruits on the plant too long, they'll grow big seeds and become bitter tasting. Ripe eggplants have shiny skin. If the skin is dull, they're past their prime, and you should pick them and throw them in the worm bin or compost heap. Use a knife or pruners to pick the fruits, leaving at least ½ inch of stem.

---

### GROWING TIPS

Eggplants (the fruits) are heavy. Stake plants individually (one stake per plant, placed next to the stem and tied) to support the plants and keep the fruits from sitting on the soil.

If you've had problems with insects, one way to thwart them is to plant groups of the same vegetable in different areas of the vegetable garden. The pests might find one group but will leave the others alone.

# OKRA *(Abelmoschus esculentus)*

Okra is a hot-weather vegetable known for its pointy pods that have a somewhat slimy texture when cooked. Although that may not sound very appetizing, okra is actually really delicious if prepared correctly. It's a key ingredient in gumbo but also tastes wonderful when brushed with olive oil and roasted or dipped in cornmeal and fried. It's easy to find frozen okra, which is fine for soups, but you'll want fresh okra for roasting or frying. Do you like to make your own pickles? Pickled okra is always the first thing to disappear off of any crudité plate I put out at an event. In addition to its versatility, the flowers of this vegetable in the mallow (hibiscus) family are pretty, so make room in the garden for it.

## ■ *Recommended Varieties*

'Clemson Spineless', 'Lee', 'Annie Oakley', and 'Cajun Delight' are all spineless varieties that grow well in the Mid-Atlantic. 'Prelude' is an open-pollinated variety (you can save the seeds) longer pods than most hybrids. 'Red Burgundy' has red, not green, pods.

## ■ *When and Where to Plant*

**Temperature:** Okra likes it hot. Don't bother planting until the soil temperature is at least 65°F to 70°F at a depth of 4 inches. That ranges from early May to early June in the Mid-Atlantic.

---

### GROWING TIPS

While few pests attack okra, there are some diseases that will take hold if the leaves of the plants stay wet and there's low air movement. To get a good harvest, allow enough space between plants for airflow. Even in raised beds, you can't cram these plants together.

Okra needs well-drained, loose soil to thrive. If you have a problem with clay, consider growing okra in a container or in a raised bed that drains well.

Because okra grows so tall, you might need to stake the plants. They'll keep growing and producing best if they stay upright, so plant them along a trellis or stake each plant individually.

In the warmest areas, you can cut okra plants back by half in mid- to late summer. They'll grow out and produce a second fall crop.

**Soil:** Rotate the planting location of okra from year to year to keep plants from suffering from soilborne diseases.

**Sun:** Full sun; plant on the north side of the garden so that the tall plants don't shade other plants reaching for the sun.

## ■ How to Plant

**Starting seeds indoors:** Not necessary; it is helpful to soak the seeds for 12 hours before planting outside to ensure good germination rates.

**Planting outside:** If planting transplants, try not to disturb the roots—okra is finicky about transplanting. Use scissors to cut the pot away from the plant, rather than yanking the plant out of the pot. Space transplants 9 to 12 inches apart. Sow seeds at a rate of one every 4 inches. Thin plants to 9- to 12-inch spacing after plants have germinated and have three sets of leaves.

## ■ How to Grow

**Water:** Allow the soil to dry out between plantings. Water deeply (so that the soil is wet to a depth of 6 to 8 inches) but infrequently.

**Fertilizer:** Fertilize once during the growing season with a balanced fertilizer.

**Pest control:** One reason to grow okra: no bad pest problems.

## ■ When and How to Harvest

Harvest okra when the pods are 2 to 3 inches long. The larger the pod, the tougher it will be, and the less tasty. Once an okra plant starts producing pods big enough to harvest, it will keep going until frost occurs or it wears itself out. Plan to pick new pods every single day. If you miss pods and they get too large, pick them off and compost them—leaving them on will signal the plant to stop producing.

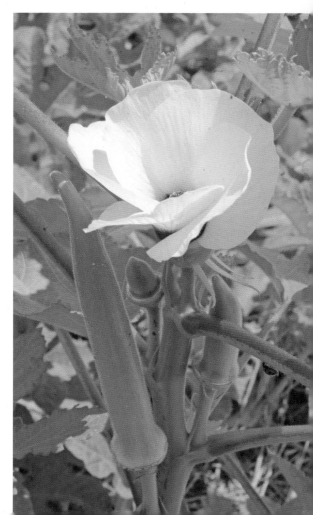

Okra fresh from the garden is best for roasting or frying.

The Mid-Atlantic is a great place to grow peppers.

# PEPPER *(Capsicum annuum)*

Like eggplants and tomatoes, peppers are members of the nightshade family. The only part of the plant that is edible is the fruit. Never eat the flowers or the leaves—they're poisonous. (Not that you probably would, but if there is one plant that you don't want to experiment with, it's peppers.) There are hundreds of varieties to grow—from bell peppers to banana peppers, from hot to sweet. As with all of the warm-season vegetables, almost every variety of pepper will grow equally well in the Mid-Atlantic. Regions that don't have enough heat hours can struggle getting peppers to fruit, but that is definitely not something we have to worry about here! So pick a potted pepper and plant it. You're almost guaranteed success. It's expensive to buy fresh peppers at the grocery store, so learning how to grow these vegetables can have a significant impact on your shopping bill.

## ■ Recommended Varieties

Any variety you select will grow well, as long as you give it the right conditions. Always look for disease resistance when selecting plant types. This will be indicated on the plant tag or seed packet. Here are some favorites to try:

**Bell pepper:** 'Keystone Resistant Giant Strain 3', 'Yolo Wonder', 'King Arthur'.
**Banana pepper:** 'Banana Supreme', 'Hy-Fry, Biscayne', 'Key Largo', 'Cubanelle', 'Gypsy', 'Hungarian Sweet Wax'.
**Hot pepper:** Red Cherry (Small), Red Cherry (Large), 'Anaheim Chili TMR 23', 'Ancho Villa', 'Early Jalopeno', 'Mitla', 'Hungarian Yellow Wax', 'Habanero'.
**Pimento:** 'Pimento Select', 'True Heart Perfection'.

One thing to note when selecting peppers is to read the "days to maturity" number on the packet. Habanero peppers can take up to 100 days to mature. If you live in the coldest areas of the Mid-Atlantic, you might not have enough frost-free days to grow those varieties.

## ■ When and Where to Plant

**Temperature:** Peppers need warm soil to grow—at least 65°F to 75°F at a depth of 4 inches. They will experience blossom drop (and lowered fruit production) if daytime temperatures are consistently over 95°F. Do not plant outside until all danger of frost has passed. Plan to plant peppers outside in late May in the warmest areas of the Mid-Atlantic and in early June in the coolest areas.

**Soil:** Peppers grow best with a soil pH of at least 6.5. Bell and sweet peppers are also heavy feeders, so add compost to the soil before planting.

**Sun:** Full sun.

## ■ When and How to Plant

**Starting seeds indoors:** It's advantageous to start seeds indoors yourself or purchase transplants so that you end up with productive plants before the real heat of summer bears down on the area. Start seeds indoors six weeks before you plan to transplant outside. You want the transplants to be at least 6 inches tall before planting outside. For strong transplants, use a heat mat placed under the seedling flat

Some bell peppers can be left on the plant longer for a red or orange color.

and grow lights 2 to 4 inches above the flat. (It is helpful to put grow lights on chains so that you can easily raise them as the plants grow.) Keep the lights on for sixteen-hour days during the entire growing period.

To get strong seedlings, follow this protocol: Sow seeds in a seedling flat with a heat mat under it. When plants sprout and have their first leaves, leave the grow lights on the plants for at least sixteen hours per day. When the first true leaves (second set of leaves) appear, transplant seedlings into 4-inch pots. Let the plants grow. Harden off the plants when all danger of frost has passed, and then plant in the garden.

**Planting outside:** Plant peppers outside when soil temperatures are at least 65°F. Plant transplants 12 inches apart.

## ■ *How to Grow*

**Water:** Bell and sweet peppers thrive with regular water. If they go through wet/dry/wet/dry cycles and/or the pH of the soil is too low, they develop blossom-end rot, a condition in which the end of the fruit opposite the stem rots. Hot peppers are one of the most drought-tolerant vegetables but benefit from watering when first planted.

**Fertilizer:** Feed peppers with a balanced fertilizer when they start blooming and again four weeks later.

**Pest control:** A huge variety of pests like to eat peppers. There are also many specific virus problems that affect these plants. Planting resistant varieties

Banana peppers are easy to grow!

**GROWING TIPS**

Use soaker hoses around pepper plants so that you can deliver consistent moisture.

Bell and sweet peppers thrive when mulched with shredded newspaper, shredded hardwood, and other organic mulches.

Stake plants individually when they grow to heights of 18 inches or taller.

Wear gloves when harvesting hot peppers.

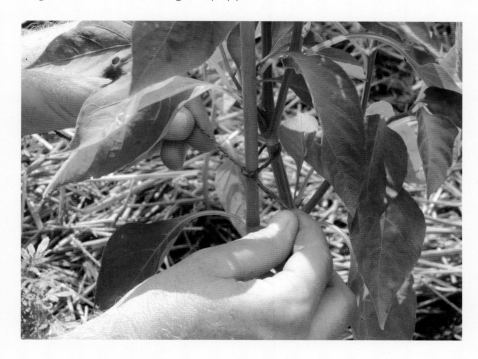

helps keep some pests under control. Growing the plants under floating row covers until they start flowering can control other pests.

## ■ *When and How to Harvest*

Read the seed packet or plant tag to see when your peppers will be ready to harvest. There will be an indication of days to maturity (after transplanting outside), as well as pictures that show you what the "finished product" looks like. Some red bell peppers are green when they're immature and turn red eventually. Some bell peppers never turn red. Hungarian wax peppers can be picked when green or red. It gets confusing. The longer peppers grow, the sweeter or hotter they get.

# POTATO *(Solanum tuberosum)*

Potatoes are easy to grow in the Mid-Atlantic, provided that you start with disease-free stock. The best way to do that is to purchase seed potatoes from local vendors. You'll plant potatoes in the spring and harvest throughout the summer.

## ■ *Recommended Varieties*

Purchasing disease-resistant and disease-free seed potatoes is important for this area. Refer to the chart below for information on desirable and resistant varieties.

### Potato Varieties Suggested for Resistance Characteristics

R=resistant, MR=moderately resistant, MS=moderately susceptible, S=susceptible, VS=very susceptible

| Variety | Late Blight | Early Blight | Common Scab |
|---|---|---|---|
| Atlantic | S | MS | MS |
| Andover | S | S | MR |
| Chieftain | S | MS | MS |
| E11-45 | S | MS | MR |
| Elba | MR | MR | MS |
| Eva | S | MS | MR |
| Katahdin | MS | MR | MS |
| Kennebec | MR | MR | MS |
| Keuka Gold | S | S | R |
| Norland | S | VS | R |
| Norvalley | S | S | MR |
| Norwis | S | S | S |
| Pike | MR | MR | R |
| Red Pontiac | S | S | S |
| Reba | S | MS | MR |
| Russet Norkotah | S | VS | MR |
| Salem | S | MS | R |
| Sebago | MR | MR | MR |
| Snowden | MS | MR | MS |
| Superior | S | S | R |
| Yukon Gold | S | VS | S |

Information provided by the Penn State Extension Service

## ■ *When and Where to Plant*

**Temperature:** Potatoes sprout when the soil temperature is between 50°F and 70°F. Plant outside in April or May in the Coastal and Piedmont regions and May or early June in the Mountain and Plateau regions.

**Soil:** Loose, well-drained soil.

**Sun:** Full sun.

Digging for potatoes is a great way for children to get involved in the garden.

## ▦ *How to Plant*

**Planting outside:** Plant potatoes 4 to 6 inches deep outside about three weeks before the last frost. Leave 12 inches between plants.

## ▦ *How to Grow*

**Water:** Keep potatoes evenly moist but not soggy. Let the soil dry out between waterings.

**Fertilizer:** Apply low-nitrogen, high-phosphorous fertilizer at the time of planting. (Bone meal works well.)

**Pest control:** Diseases are the main problem. Start with disease-free seed potatoes. There are a variety of pests that attack potatoes. If you suspect a problem, contact your cooperative extension.

**Hilling:** Potatoes need to be "hilled," which is to say that as the plants grow, you'll want to mound the soil around the plant stem so that about 6 to 12 inches of growth remains above ground.

## ▦ *How to Harvest*

You can harvest early potatoes by carefully removing some of the soil from around the stem and feeling around for immature potatoes. The rest of the potatoes are ready to harvest when the tops of the plants start dying back in late summer.

---

### GROWING TIPS

Don't let the soil around potatoes stay soggy.

Keep up with hilling—check plants every two to three weeks as they grow.

# SUMMER SQUASH *(Cucurbita pepo)*

If you grow more than two or three summer squash plants, you will have to engage in what I like to call the "zucchini drop and dash." This is when you leave bags of summer squash on porches, in unlocked cars, and anywhere anyone isn't looking, really. These plants are prolific if you can keep the squash vine borers away from them. They also grow really fast. Forget to pick a zucchini one day, and you're playing squash bowling the next day with the giant bowling-pin-sized fruits. Luckily there are as many ways to eat summer squash as there are fruits produced on each plant.

## ■ *Recommended Varieties*

Summer squashes include all of the thin-skinned squashes that are suitable for eating cooked or raw. Yellow crookneck varieties are popular, as are typical dark green zucchini plants. You can grow pattypan squash, which look like little yellow and white space ships, or round zucchini that look like pool balls. Try these varieties:

**Yellow straightneck:** 'Saffron', 'Seneca Butterbar'.
**Yellow crookneck:** 'Dixie', 'Multipik'.
**Zucchini:** 'Costata Romanesco', 'Spineless Beauty', 'Eight Ball'(round).
**Pattypan:** 'Sunburst', 'Peter Pan'.

When possible, read the seed packets to purchase varieties that are resistant to cucumber mosaic virus, powdery mildew, and downy mildew.

Harvest summer squash right after the flower on the end of the fruit wilts.

## When and Where to Plant

**Temperature:** Squashes need warm soil to grow. Plant outside when soil temperatures are at least 65°F. This can range from early May to early June in the Mid-Atlantic. Keep your soil thermometer handy.

**Soil:** Squashes grow best in a pH of 6.0 to 6.5. Add compost to the soil before planting. If the soil test shows low boron levels, scratch 1 teaspoon of borax into the soil per plant.

**Sun:** Full sun.

## How to Plant

**Starting seeds indoors:** Squash plants are difficult to transplant. If you want to get a jump on the season, start seeds indoors two weeks before you want to plant outdoors. Plant the seeds in peat pots or biodegradable pots that you can plant directly in the ground without removing the plants.

**Planting outside:** Sow seeds outside when soil temperatures are at least 65°F. Plant two to three seeds per hole, 1 inch deep. When seedlings are 3 inches tall, use scissors to thin to two plants per 12 inches. As plants grow, you can further reduce to one plant per 18 or 24 inches. (Overplanting slightly gives you more plants to work with if you have problems with pests.)

## How to Grow

**Water:** Keep squashes evenly moist. It helps if you mulch the garden after the plants germinate.

**Fertilizer:** Sidedress with a balanced fertilizer every three weeks during the growing season.

**Pest control:** Squash bugs, squash vine borers, cucumber beetles, and squash beetles plague squash plants. Use row covers when plants are young to protect plants from the flying pests. You can raise the covers for two hours in the early morning a few days a week to allow insects to reach the flowers for pollination.

## When and How to Harvest

Once summer squash plants start producing, you need to check the plants daily for fruits to harvest. Summer squash tastes better when harvested young. You can even harvest with the flowers still hanging on to the ends of the fruits.

# TOMATILLO *(Physalis ixocarpa)*

Sometimes known as the "husk tomato," tomatillos are green fruits that grow inside a papery shell. You can use them fresh, roasted, or sautéed. Tomatillos have a slightly tart flavor, but cooking them brings out some sweetness. A few tomatillo seeds go a long way because tomatillos are ridiculously easy to grow from seed. In fact, they're easier to grow from seed than from transplants. They are also prolific producers that reseed all over the place.

## Recommended Varieties

'Toma Verde' is a smaller, sweeter variety of tomatillo. 'De Milpa' is a lavender-colored heirloom tomatillo. Purple is a variety that is purple inside and out. Don't get overly concerned with selecting a variety, though. Plant a tomatillo seed, and it will grow.

## ■ *When and Where to Plant*

**Temperature:** Tomatillos like it hot. Plant seeds (or transplants) outside when the soil temperature is at least 60°F. This ranges from mid-May to early June in the Mid-Atlantic. Use your soil thermometer to see when it's time to plant.

**Soil:** Tomatillos aren't picky plants but will grow best in well-drained soil. If you have clay soil, amend with compost before planting.

**Sun:** Full sun.

## ■ *How to Plant*

**Starting seeds indoors:** You only need to plant tomatillo seeds indoors if you grow them in the cooler mountainous regions. Start seeds inside six weeks before you plan to plant outside. For strong seedlings, use a heat mat under the seedling flat and grow lights 2 inches above the plants (moved up as they grow).

**Planting outside:** Plant seeds outside when the soil temperature is at least 60°F. Cover lightly with seed-starting mix, and keep moist. When the plants are 3 inches tall, thin to allow 12 inches between plants.

## ■ *How to Grow*

**Water:** Keep tomatillos evenly moist. Wet/dry/wet/dry cycles can cause blossom-end rot.

**Fertilizer:** Sidedress with a balanced fertilizer four weeks after planting.

**Pest control:** Keep an eye out for pests that attack tomatoes, such as tomato hornworms, aphids, and cutworms. You can protect plants from cutworms by wrapping the bottom 3 inches of the stems with newspaper.

## ■ *When and How to Harvest*

Pick tomatillos off the plants when the husks start to dry out and turn light brown.

---

### GROWING TIPS

Place tomato cages around individual plants to keep them from flopping over.

For a bushier plant, pinch off the top of the plant to encourage side sprouts.

If growing tomatillos from seed, hill the soil up around the bottom 6 inches of the stem as the plant grows. If planting transplants, plant 4 or 5 inches deep to encourage rooting from the stem.

# TOMATO *(Lycopersicon esculentum)*

Nothing beats the taste of a fresh-picked tomato from the garden. I grew up not even liking tomatoes until my eighth-grade teacher dropped off a bag at my house for me to try. (We became gardening friends after I "graduated" middle school.) I was hooked. Today's commercial tomatoes are grown for their ability to withstand shipping, not for their flavor. Tomatoes that you purchase in the grocery store have been picked when still green and gassed with the plant hormone ethylene to get them to turn red. No wonder I didn't like them. A farmers' market tomato is closer to the "real thing," but if you want to can, dry, or cook with massive amounts of fresh tomatoes, the only thing to do is grow them yourself.

A prolific tomato plant can produce almost more fruits than you can use. However, there are so many pests and diseases that plague tomatoes that it is always a good idea to overplant. You can always find a home for fresh garden tomatoes if you have too many.

## ■ *Recommended Varieties*

There are three main types of tomatoes available. Patio tomatoes are small, basically dwarf, tomatoes that grow in raised beds or containers. Most patio tomatoes have small cherry- or grape-sized fruits. Determinate tomatoes are still large vines, but they eventually stop growing taller and just grow more fruits. Indeterminate tomatoes are vining plants that will grow forever if not cut back. Wild tomatoes (from which all cultivated tomatoes are descended) are vining plants that can grow 10 feet or more!

The key to success with tomatoes is to start with varieties that have a proven track record in the Mid-Atlantic. Hot, humid summer weather is challenging for plants. It provides a wonderful environment for pests and diseases to flourish. Most of the tomato varieties that grow well here are resistant to some or most of the common diseases that plague tomatoes.

Read the seed packets and plant labels to determine disease resistance. Plants resistant to fusarium wilt will have F, FF, or FFF after the cultivar name. VFN on the label indicates that the plants are resistant to verticillium wilt, fusarium wilt, and root knot nematodes; VFNT indicates resistance to these three diseases, plus tobacco mosaic virus. Plants resistant to tomato spotted wilt virus have TSWV on the plant tags.

High-performing tomatoes for the Mid-Atlantic include 'Better Boy', 'Early Girl', 'First Lady', 'Delicious', and 'Big Beef'. Cherry tomatoes including 'Sugar Snack' and 'Sweet Million' grow well in the Mid-Atlantic.

'Yellow pear' tomatoes are indeterminate tomatoes that produce tons of yellow, lightbulb-shaped grape tomatoes. Two of these plants will give you enough tomatoes for every salad you eat all summer long.

Check at your local farmers' markets to see what tomatoes those growers recommend. They'll have experience growing for market in your area.

## When and Where to Plant

**Temperature:** Tomatoes are absolute heat lovers. Don't bother planting until the soil temperature is at least 65°F and nighttime temperatures are regularly at least 65°F to 70°F. Plant outside in mid- to late May in the Coastal Plain and Piedmont, and in early June in the Mountain and Plateau areas.

**Soil:** The soil pH should be 6.0 to 7.0. If you have more acidic soil, add lime before planting. Mix in slow-release, organic fertilizer such as Plant-tone before planting, as well.

**Sun:** Full sun.

## How to Plant

**Starting seeds indoors:** Start seeds indoors six weeks before you want to plant tomatoes outdoors. Use a heat mat and grow lights elevated 2 inches above the plants to grow strong transplants. Harden off plants before planting them in the garden.

**Planting outside:** Plant transplants outside after hardening off. Space plants 18 inches apart, and plant transplants 5 inches deep to encourage rooting from the stem and a deep root system.

## How to Grow

**Water:** Tomatoes need steady, consistent moisture in order to avoid blossom-end rot (the end of the fruit opposite from the stem rots), a cultural

For best results, keep tomatoes consistently and evenly watered.

## GROWING TIPS

Place tomato cages and supports when you plant the plants. It is easier to do this when the plants are small than after they start growing. You can also stake individual plants with metal or wood stakes placed next to the stem and tied to the plant.

Chipmunks and squirrels will take bites out of tomatoes if they're having a hard time finding water. You can spray tomatoes with repellents to protect fruits.

Pinch suckers (sprouts growing from between the main stem and productive branches) to direct resources to the main fruiting branches.

If you live in the colder areas of the Mid-Atlantic, plant fast-maturing varieties, and keep an eye on the weather. Use frost protection if temperatures are supposed to drop below 50°F after you've planted your tomatoes.

Yellow pear tomatoes are prolific producers.

Cracking fruit is caused by uneven watering. Use soaker hoses with tomatoes to avoid this problem.

problem (caused by the gardener's plant care, not by a pest) that arises when calcium is deficient in the soil or watering is inconsistent. Use soaker hoses to make it easier to water tomatoes deeply.

**Fertilizer:** Avoid high-nitrogen fertilizer, which can cause more leaf growth than flower development. Fertilize with a 0-5-0 fertilizer when plants start flowering.

**Pest control:** Almost every pest alive enjoys eating tomatoes. Growing resistant varieties helps avoid many pest problems. Keep an eye out for tomato hornworms. You'll know them when you see them. They're big green worms as large as your thumb. Pick them off and squash them.

## ■ *When and How to Harvest*

Tomatoes are ripe when you need little effort to pull them off the plant. Leave tomatoes on the plant for as long as possible for the sweetest fruits.

# WINTER SQUASH *(Cucurbita* spp.*)*

Winter squash grows in much the same way as summer squash, but the fruits take longer to mature. They also keep longer in storage. Popular winter squash varieties include pumpkins, acorn squash, and butternut squash. The term *winter squash* is a bit of a misnomer here, as winter squashes are ready for harvest between July and September, depending on when they were planted. You do not need to leave them in the garden until the weather cools off.

## ■ *Recommended Varieties*

**Winter squash:** 'Table King' Bush Acorn, 'Early Butternut', 'Vegetable Spaghetti', Hubbard Types, 'Celebration', 'Delicata'.

**Pumpkins:** Pumpkins are divided into different categories, including carving (large), pie (small and sweet), and gourds or decorative novelty. Try these varieties:

**Carving:** 'Autumn Gold', 'Ghost Rider', 'Jack o'Lantern', 'Howden', 'Magic Lantern', 'Merlin', 'Spirit'.

**Pie:** 'Amish Pie', 'Small Sugar'.

**Giant:** 'Big Max', 'Big Moon'.

**Novelty:** 'Baby Boo', 'Jack Be Little', 'Lumina', 'Prizewinner'.

## ■ *When and Where to Plant*

**Temperature:** Squashes need warm soil to grow. Plant outside when soil temperatures are at least 65°F. This can range from mid-May to early June in the Mid-Atlantic. Use a soil thermometer to take the temperature of the soil before planting.

**Soil:** Squashes grow best in a pH of 6.0 to 7.5. Add compost to the soil before planting. If the soil test shows low boron levels, scratch 1 teaspoon of borax into the soil per plant.

**Sun:** Full sun.

---

### GROWING TIPS

Keep fruits from rotting while they grow by raising them up off the ground on planting flats or crates.

Mulch around the plants to keep the roots cool, keep the soil moist, and minimize weeds.

Winter squash plants are big and need a lot of room. You can build a sturdy trellis from pipe and wire and train them to climb. If you do this, you might need to support the fruits in homemade slings as they grow.

## ■ *How to Plant*

**Starting seeds indoors:** Squash plants are difficult to transplant. If you want to get a jump on the season, start seeds indoors two weeks before you want to plant outdoors. Plant the seeds in peat pots or other biodegradable pots that you can plant directly in the ground without removing the plants.

**Planting outside:** Sow seeds outside when soil temperatures are at least 65°F. Plant two to three seeds per hole, 1 inch deep. When seedlings are 3 inches tall, use scissors to thin to two plants per 12 inches. As plants grow, you can further reduce to one plant per 24 or 48 inches. (Overplanting slightly gives you more plants to work with if you have problems with pests.)

Winter squash can be grown as an edible or as a decorative gourd.

## ■ *How to Grow*

**Water:** Keep squashes evenly moist. It helps if you mulch the garden after the plants germinate.

**Fertilizer:** Sidedress with a balanced fertilizer every three weeks during the growing season. Apply calcium nitrate at a rate of 2 pounds per 100 feet of row to the soil around the base of each plant when the plants start flowering.

**Pest control:** Squash bugs, squash vine borers, cucumber beetles, and Mexican bean beetles plague squash plants. Use row covers when plants are young to protect plants from the flying pests. You can raise the covers for two hours in the early morning a few days a week to allow insects to reach the flowers for pollination.

## ■ *When and How to Harvest*

Winter squashes are ready to harvest when the skin has thickened and is dull, not shiny. Cut squashes from the vine, leaving 1 inch of stem. Wipe the soil off the fruits, and then use a clean cloth dipped in chlorine or a dilute bleach solution to wipe them down to kill any bacteria on the outside.

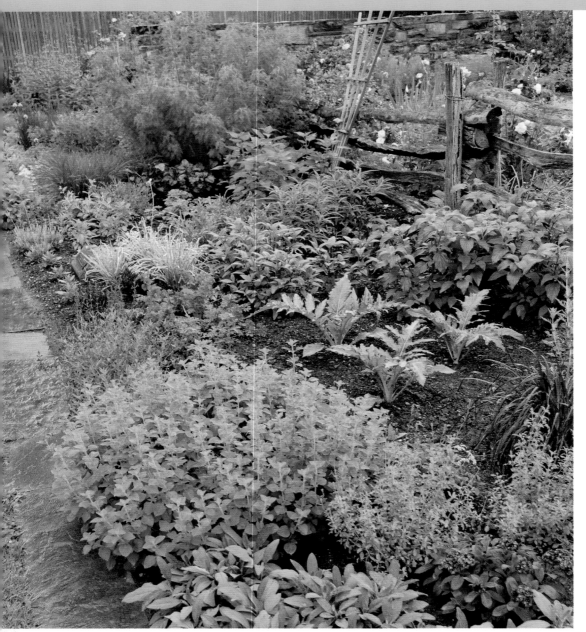

# Warm-Season Herbs

Many of the herbs that flourish during warm weather are also cold hardy, but they don't grow and thrive during the cooler weather. For all of these herbs to produce fresh growth that's ideal for cooking, they need full sun and warm temperatures.

Some warm-season herbs are perennials, while others are annuals. Perennial herbs are ideal for planting in the flower garden or right outside your kitchen door. I find that I use what's near the kitchen more frequently than what's out in the "back 40" where my vegetables are planted. I do find that it's easier to maintain annual herbs if they're growing with the vegetables. The annual warm-season herbs usually need more water than the perennials.

A note about planting times for these herbs: you can plant any and all of the warm season herbs at the same time that you plant any warm season vegetables. Perennial herbs can go outside earlier than tender annual herbs.

# BASIL *(Ocimum basilicum)*

What's a fresh garden tomato without basil? Some people love making their own pesto from bunches of this prolific herb. While pesto isn't my cup of tea, I love basil with tomatoes and eggplants, with squash, in salads, or on toast with fresh mozzarella. Basil is a perfect complement to warm-season vegetables. It's a true warm-season herb that thrives in hot weather. It's easy to grow and comes in a variety of different flavors and varieties.

## ■ *Recommended Varieties*

There are so many varieties of basil. All will grow equally well if planted when it is hot outside. Try lemon basil for a different flavor in cocktails and lemonade. Sweet basil is the classic pesto basil variety. You can also find chocolate basil and cinnamon basil. Largeleaf Italian basil is a good all-around variety. 'African Blue' is a fairly cold-tolerant basil that you can grow on a sunny windowsill in the garage during winter. 'Greek Columnar' is a nonflowering variety of basil.

**GROWING TIPS**

Cut the flowers off basil to encourage more production of fragrant leaves.

If basil plants get too leggy, just chop the plant back by two-thirds to one-half, water, and fertilize well.

## ■ *When and Where to Plant*

**Temperature:** Plant outside when nighttime temperatures are consistently at least 70°F. You can plant basil outside in the Coastal Plain in April, in the Piedmont in May and in the Mountain and Plateau areas in June.

**Soil:** Basil grows best in soil with a pH of 5.5 to 7.0. Add compost to the soil before planting.

**Sun:** Full sun.

## ■ *How to Plant*

**Starting seeds indoors:** Start seeds indoors two weeks before planting outdoors.

**Planting outside:** Plant transplants outside, 12 inches apart.

## ■ *How to Grow*

**Water:** Basil isn't a heavy drinker, but keep it evenly moist.

**Fertilizer:** As with most herbs, basil doesn't require a lot of extra fertilizer. In fact, extra fertilizer will make basil less fragrant.

**Pest control:** Japanese beetles and slugs are the most problematic pests for basil. There's not much you can do about Japanese beetles, but you can spread diatomaceous earth around the base of each plant to keep slugs from munching.

## ■ *When and How to Harvest*

Snip leaves off the top of the plant in the morning. Basil is a forgiving and fast-growing plant. You can chop off any piece of the plant, and it will grow back.

# CHIVES *(Allium schoenoprasum)*

Chives are perennial herbs. This robust plant forms large clumps that can be divided and shared with friends. You can use chives in pastas, fresh salsas, and roasted or grilled dishes.

Both the flowers and the stems of chives are edible.

## ■ *Recommended Varieties*

There aren't really different varieties of chives. Plant whatever you can find at the garden center.

## ■ *When and Where to Plant*

**Temperature:** Plant chives outside in spring when soil temperatures are at least 60°F.

**Soil:** Chives are not picky about soil, but will grow best in well-draining soils.

**Sun:** Full sun.

## ■ *How to Plant*

**Starting seeds indoors:** Start seeds indoors one month before planting outside.

**Planting outside:** Chives are easy to grow from seed. Sow seeds outdoors and cover with seed-starting mix. Keep seeds moist while germinating.

## ■ *How to Grow*

**Water:** Keep the soil evenly moist. Give extra water after cutting back.

**Fertilizer:** No extra fertilizer is needed.

**Pest control:** Chives have no pest problems.

## ■ *When and How to Harvest*

Keep chives producing leaves by cutting sections of the plant back to 3 inches tall once the whole plant is 6 to 8 inches tall. (Don't cut the entire plant back all the way to the ground.)

Chives are one of the earliest herbs to appear in the garden in spring.

**GROWING TIPS**

You can let chives flower, or you can cut the flowers off if you want the plants to keep producing leaves. The flowers are edible.

# MARJORAM *(Origanum majorana)*

Marjoram is a perennial semiwoody herb in the Mid-Atlantic. Add marjoram leaves to chicken dishes, soups, stews, salads, and salad dressings. This versatile herb adds zing to almost any meal, and you're much more likely to use it frequently if you grow your own plants. Make room in the sunny perennial garden for this herb, because you'll want it to stick around.

## ■ Recommended Varieties

There are not a lot of different marjoram varieties. For the most success, purchase plants that have been grown outdoors locally and are well adapted to local soils and temperatures.

## ■ When and Where to Plant

**Temperature:** Transplant outside when all danger of frost has passed.

**Soil:** Marjoram is well adapted to grow in most any soil but does best in well-drained soil.

**Sun:** Full sun.

Marjoram is often confused with oregano, but marjoram has a gentler, sweeter flavor.

Let some of the marjoram plants flower to attract pollinators to the vegetable garden.

## ■ *How to Plant*

**Starting seeds indoors:** You can start seeds indoors or sow directly outside. It is easier to just grow from transplants.

**Planting outside:** Space plants 8 inches apart. You really only need one or two marjoram plants, and they can be worked into the flower garden.

## ■ *How to Grow*

**Water:** Water while the plant is getting established. Then water at the same rate you'd water the perennial garden.

**Fertilizer:** Feed once a year in spring with balanced organic fertilizer.

**Pest control:** Aphids and spider mites can attack marjoram if there's a severe drought in the area and plants get stressed. You can prevent these pest problems by watering plants during dry times.

## ■ *When and How to Harvest*

Snip off the tender new growth for use in fresh salads. You can use woodier, older growth in soups and roasts.

**GROWING TIP**

To keep plants producing leaves, snip off the flowers before they open.

Grow mint in a pot to prevent it from taking over the garden.

# MINT *(Mentha* spp.*)*

There are two types of perennial mint commonly grown in the Mid-Atlantic: peppermint (*Mentha* × *piperita*) and spearmint (*Mentha spicata*). Both types are so prolific that they're practically weeds. If you want to grow mint, I'd advise growing it in a pot where it can't escape and take over the entire garden.

## ■ *Recommended Varieties*

'Kentucky Colonel' is a spearmint and the official mint of the Kentucky Derby. It tastes great in mint juleps. 'Chocolate' mint really does taste like a YORK Peppermint Pattie. There are many different varieties of mint. Experiment!

## When and Where to Plant

**Temperature:** Plant mint after all danger of frost has passed.
**Soil:** Mint is widely adaptable to all soils.
**Sun:** Full sun to partial shade.

## How to Plant

**Starting seeds indoors:** You don't really grow mint from seed. Grow it from cuttings. If you know anyone who has mint, just cut a few stems and stick them in water to root.
**Planting outside:** Once the cuttings have rooted, plant them outside in a large pot.

**GROWING TIP**

It bears repeating: mint can be highly invasive. Grow it in a pot.

## How to Grow

**Water:** Mint is a somewhat heavy drinker. Keep plants moist.
**Fertilizer:** No extra fertilizer is needed.
**Pest control:** Mint has no pest problems.

## When and How to Harvest

Cut off the tops of the plants to use. Stick in a glass of water until you need to use the leaves.

Children will appreciate the many different varieties of mint.

# OREGANO *(Origanum vulgare* subsp. *hirtum)*

Oregano is a perennial herb that's so easy to grow, it's almost a weed. Thankfully, though part of the mint family, it doesn't spread as crazily as mint. Oregano grows in large clumps.

## ▪ Recommended Varieties

There are a few different varieties of oregano but not enough to recommend one over the other.

## ▪ When and Where to Plant

**Temperature:** Plant oregano outside after danger of frost has passed.
**Soil:** Oregano grows best in soil with a pH of 6.5 to 7.5.
**Sun:** Full sun.

## ▪ How to Plant

**Starting seeds indoors:** You can start seeds indoors. Sprinkle them on top of the soil, water them, and cover the seedling flat with a piece of plastic wrap to keep the seeds moist as the plants germinate.

**Planting outside:** You can also sow seeds outside directly on top of the soil and use a piece of plastic wrap to keep them moist. However, it is just as easy to buy a couple of plants from the garden center and call it a day. You definitely don't need more than one or two.

Oregano is often known as the "pizza" herb.

Growing oregano in a pot ensures it won't hog all of the space in your vegetable garden.

## ▓ *How to Grow*

**Water:** No extra water is needed after plants have established themselves.

**Fertilizer:** No extra fertilizer is needed.

**Pest control:** Aphids and spider mites may attack oregano when it's very dry outside. Water the plant if your region is experiencing drought. The insects will eventually go away. It's almost impossible to kill oregano.

## ▓ *When and How to Harvest*

Leaves are most fragrant just before the flowers open, but you can snip leaves off to use at any time.

---

**GROWING TIP**

The primary objective with oregano is to keep it from taking over the garden. Even though it is a clumping perennial herb, the stems will form roots and spread if allowed to. Periodically cut the entire plant back. It will grow out amazingly fast.

# ROSEMARY *(Rosmarinus officinalis)*

Rosemary is a woody, evergreen perennial herb that grows to be a medium-sized shrub in most of the Mid-Atlantic. It is native to the Mediterranean and thrives in well-drained soil. It's easy to grow once established and so fun to cook with. You can use fresh rosemary when roasting meats and vegetables. Rosemary twigs make excellent kebab sticks for grilling. Save a corner of the garden for this tasty herb.

## ■ Recommended Varieties

To keep rosemary growing in your Mid-Atlantic garden, you need to plant cold-hardy varieties. The U.S. National Arboretum recommends these varieties for excellent cold hardiness:

R. *officinalis* 'Albus'          R. *officinalis* 'Logee's Light Blue'
R. *officinalis* 'Bendenen Blue'  R. *officinalis* 'Miss Jessup's Upright'
R. *officinalis* 'Goodwin Creek'  R. *officinalis* 'Russian River'
R. *officinalis* 'Herb Cottage'   R. *officinalis* 'Salem'

## ■ When and Where to Plant

**Temperature:** Plant transplants outside after danger of frost has passed, for best establishment.

**Soil:** Rosemary is widely adaptable to many different soil types but does need well-drained soil.

**Sun:** Full sun.

## ■ How to Plant

**Starting seeds indoors:** Not recommended.

**Planting outside:** It is much easier to grow rosemary from transplants than to attempt to grow it from seed. Plant transplants outside where they'll have room to grow to be 3 feet wide and 3 feet tall over time.

---

**GROWING TIPS**

Leave rosemary alone. If you baby it, you're more likely to kill it. Once it is established, don't water it unless your area is experiencing a severe drought. Don't feed, as that promotes weak growth that's susceptible to pests.

## ■ *When and How to Grow*

**Water:** No extra water is needed once plants are established.

**Fertilizer:** No extra fertilizer is needed.

**Pest control:** Mealybugs and scale are the two pests that afflict rosemary. Use horticultural oil to treat the plant for these pests.

## ■ *When and How to Harvest*

Cut pieces of rosemary at any time of the year to use for cooking. The young tips are best for mixing into fresh salads. The rest of the plant is good for use in soups, stews, or roasting.

Rosemary is equally prized for its beautiful winter flowers as it is for its fragrant leaves.

Sage grows best from cuttings.

# SAGE *(Salvia officinalis)*

The sage that we use in cooking is called "culinary sage," and all varieties are from the *officinalis* species of salvia. This tough perennial is extremely hardy but needs well-drained soil in order to grow. In the Mid-Atlantic, because perennial garden sage doesn't die back to the ground every year, the stems can become woody, and the plant can start producing fewer fragrant leaves. If you have an old sage plant, cut it back to spur on new growth.

## ■ *Recommended Varieties*

Beyond the straight species of garden sage, there are many varieties with interesting colors of leaves, increased cold hardiness, and other desirable characteristics. 'Berggarten' sage is a hardier, more compact variety than the straight species of sage. Purple sage is also a garden sage that has deep purple leaves. 'Tricolor' sage has leaves that are purple, green, and white. It is decorative and useful. 'Woodcote' sage has variegated green and white leaves.

**GROWING TIPS**

For more fragrant leaves, cut off sage flowers when they appear. The plant will channel more of its energy into leaf production, which is the part you cook with, anyway.

Replant garden sage every three to four years for fresh, new growth. (You can take cuttings off your existing plants for replanting.)

## When and Where to Plant

**Temperature:** Garden sage only produces new leaves worth cooking with when the weather is warm.

**Soil:** Plant in well-drained soil.

**Sun:** Garden sage needs full sun to be most productive and for leaves to be their most fragrant.

## How to Plant

**Starting seeds indoors:** Sage is easier to grow from cuttings than from seed. To take cuttings, use pruners or snips to cut off the top 4 inches of tender new growth. Strip off leaves from the lower half and stick it in a glass of water. Once the plant has rooted, plant it in a 4-inch pot and allow it to root into the soil. Once the plant has established good roots (you can pull up on the plant without uprooting it), transplant it outside.

**Planting outside:** Plant outside when all danger of frost has passed, for best establishment.

## How to Grow

**Water:** Once established, sage needs no extra water. In fact, extra water can actually harm the plant.

**Fertilizer:** Sage does not usually need extra fertilizer, but a once-a-year feeding in spring with a slow-release, balanced fertilizer won't hurt the plant.

**Pest control:** Slugs may attack sage when conditions are wetter than usual, and spider mites can be a problem during times of extreme drought. Both problems will go away on their own, eventually.

## When and How to Harvest

Cut stems or individual leaves to use when cooking.

# TARRAGON *(Artemisia dracunculus)*

Tarragon is another herb that you're much more likely to use if you grow it. I always put fistfuls of leaves in chicken noodle soup. The fragrant, tasty herb really jazzes up an otherwise bland dish. This perennial herb is hardy in the Mid-Atlantic and is semievergreen. You can harvest fresh leaves year-round in the warmest areas of this region.

## ◼ *Recommended Varieties*

French tarragon is the more flavorful type but it struggles in areas with long, hot summers. If you have trouble growing this plant, try Mexican tarragon, *Tagetes lucida.*

## ◼ *When and Where to Plant*

**Temperature:** Plant tarragon transplants outside after danger of frost has passed.

**Soil:** Tarragon grows best in soil with a pH of 6.0 to 7.0.

**Sun:** Full sun to partial shade.

Tarragon can be harvested year-round.

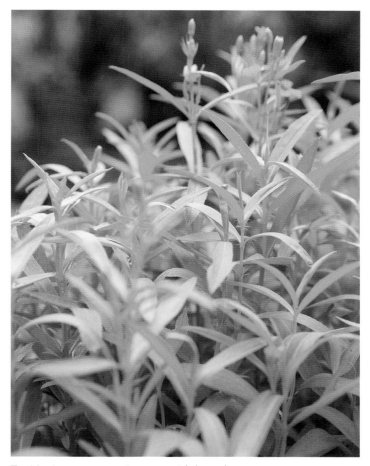

**GROWING TIP**

Plant tarragon in the vegetable garden to keep pests away from other plants.

Try Mexican tarragon in areas with long, hot summers.

## How to Plant

**Starting seeds indoors:** You can't grow French tarragon from seed, only from cuttings. Take cuttings in early spring and root them before planting outside or buy plants from the garden center.

**Planting outside:** Plant outside, allowing 12 to 18 inches between plants.

## How to Grow

**Water:** Tarragon requires an average amount of water. Water tarragon when you water your annual flowers.

**Fertilizer:** No fertilizer is necessary.

**Pest control:** There are no pests that regularly attack tarragon.

## When and How to Harvest

Cut branches in order to use the leaves in cooking. Leave at least 6 inches on the plant when cutting branches to use.

Fresh or dried, thyme makes a great flavoring for meats or vinegars.

# THYME *(Thymus vulgaris)*

Thyme is a perennial herb that is hardy in zones 5–9. There are over a hundred varieties of thyme. Thyme is indispensible for cooking savory dishes. Use it in everything from roast chicken to vegetable soup to shortbread cookies. If you're interested in making your own flavored vinegars, thyme is a good herb to try. Thyme can be cut back or replanted every few years for fresh new growth.

## ■ *Recommended Varieties*

There are so many varieties of thyme, including lemon and lime thyme! Try different varieties to see what does well in your garden. There's no need to search out specific types of thyme—just browse the garden center and see what's available.

## ■ *When and Where to Plant*

**Temperature:** Thyme grows best in warm temperatures. Plant thyme plants outside after all danger of frost has passed, for best results.
**Soil:** Thyme needs well-drained soil to grow. It will rot if kept consistently wet.
**Sun:** Full sun.

**GROWING TIPS**

If you have heavy clay soil that drains poorly, grow thyme in a pot. Plant thyme in the garden along with other vegetables to help repel pests.

## How to Plant

**Starting seeds indoors:** Not recommended.

**Planting outside:** It is much easier to grow thyme from cuttings than it is to grow it from seed. Root cuttings by snipping off 4-inch pieces of fresh, green growth from a plant. Strip the leaves off the lower half and place it in a cup of water. Once the plant has developed roots, plant it in a 4-inch pot. When the plant has rooted in, transplant it outside in full sun in well-drained soil.

## How to Grow

**Water:** Thyme does not need extra water once established.

**Fertilizer:** Fertilize once a year in spring with a balanced fertilizer.

**Pest control:** Aphids and spider mites will attack the plant if it is stressed—usually from too much water. Fungal diseases and root rot are also problems if the soil is too wet.

## When and How to Harvest

Thyme leaves are most fragrant if they are cut before the plant flowers. Keep cutting back the top 4 to 6 inches of growth to stimulate fresh, new growth, which is best for cooking.

Harvest thyme before the flowers appear.

# RESOURCES

This list is not comprehensive, but it includes numerous sources to get you going in your search for more information, plant suppliers, and local seed growers.

## Nurseries and Plant Suppliers

### Seeds

**Southern Exposure Seed Exchange**
(seeds, sweet potato slips, garlic bulbs)
www.southernexposure.com/
PO Box 460
Mineral, VA 23117
E-mail: gardens@southernexposure.com
Phone: 540-894-9480
Fax: 540-894-9481

**Seeds for the South**
(untreated heirloom vegetable, herb, tomato, and pepper seeds
www.seedsforthesouth.com/
Vegetable Seed Warehouse
P.O. Box 13741
Charleston, SC 29422
E-mail: Orders@vegetableseedwarehouse.com

**Penny's Tomatoes**
www.pennystomatoes.com/
3904 Kensington Ct.
Myrtle Beach, SC 29577
Email: penny@pennystomatoes.com
Phone: 843-626-4507
Fax: 843-626-4507

**Pepper Joe's, Inc.**
www.pepperjoe.com/
725 Carolina Farm Blvd.
Myrtle Beach, SC 29579
Email: pepperjoe1@sc.rr.com
Phone: 843-742-5116

**Sow True Seed**
(herbs, vegetables, flowers, bulbs and tubers, cover crops and grains)
www.sowtrueseed.com
146 Church Street
Asheville, NC 28801
Email: info@sowtrue.com
Phone: 828-254-0708
Fax: 828-254-0708

### Fruit Trees

**Stark Bro's**
www.starkbros.com/
11523 Highway NN
Louisiana, MO 63353
While Stark Bro's ships around the United States, they have a quality product and get good feedback from customers.
Email: info@starkbros.com
Phone: 573-754-3113

## *Websites*

### Frost Tables

http://cdo.ncdc.noaa.gov/climatenormals/clim20supp1/states
  Find the first and last frost dates for your specific city.

### USDA Plant Hardiness Zone Map

http://planthardiness.ars.usda.gov
  You can click on your state and locate the hardiness zone for your individual area.

## *Books*

*Beginner's Illustrated Guide to Gardening: Techniques to Help You Get Started*, by Katie Elzer-Peters
If you're a completely new gardener, pick up my other book, which is filled with step-by-step
  instructions for many of the most important gardening tasks. (It covers vegetable gardening
  and landscape maintenance.) Starting with a good foundation will help you be a more
  successful gardener.

# GLOSSARY

**Acidic soil:** On a soil pH scale of 0 to 14, acidic soil has a pH lower than 5.5. Most garden plants prefer a soil a bit on the acidic side.

**Afternoon sun:** A garden receiving afternoon sun typically has full sun from 1:00 to 5:00 p.m. daily, with more shade during the morning hours.

**Alkaline soil:** On a soil pH scale of 0 to 14, alkaline soil has a pH higher than 7.0. Many desert plants thrive in slightly alkaline soils.

**Annual:** A plant that germinates (sprouts), flowers, and dies within one year or season (spring, summer, winter, or fall) is an annual.

***Bacillus thuringiensis* (B.t.):** *B.t.* is an organic pest control based on naturally occurring soil bacteria, often used to control harmful caterpillars such as cutworms, leaf rollers, and webworms.

**Balled and burlapped (B&B):** This phrase describes plants that have been grown in field nursery rows, dug up with their soil intact, wrapped with burlap, and tied with twine. Most of the plants sold balled and burlapped are large evergreen plants and deciduous trees.

**Bare root:** Bare-root plants are those that are shipped dormant, without being planted in soil or having soil around their roots. Roses are often shipped bare root.

**Beneficial insects:** These insects perform valuable services such as pollination and pest control. Ladybugs, soldier beetles, and some bees are examples.

**Biennial:** A plant that blooms during its second year and then dies is a biennial.

**Bolting:** This is a process when a plant switches from leaf growth to producing flowers and seeds. Bolting often occurs quite suddenly and is usually undesirable, because the plant usually dies shortly after bolting.

**Brown materials:** A part of a well-balanced compost pile, brown materials include high-carbon materials such as brown leaves and grass, woody plant stems, dryer lint, and sawdust.

**Bud:** The bud is an undeveloped shoot nestled between the leaf and the stem that will eventually produce a flower or plant branch.

**Bulb:** A bulb is a plant with a large, rounded underground storage organ formed by the plant stem and leaves. Examples are tulips, daffodils, and hyacinths. Bulbs that flower in spring are typically planted in fall.

**Bush:** *See* shrub.

**Cane:** A stem on a fruit shrub; usually blackberry or raspberry stems are called canes, but blueberry stems can also be referred to as canes.

**Central leader:** The term for the center trunk of a fruit tree.

**Chilling hours:** Hours when the air temperature is below 45°F; chilling hours are related to fruit production.

**Common name:** A name that is generally used to identify a plant in a particular region, as opposed to its botanical name, which is standard throughout the world; for example, the common name for *Echinacea purpurea* is "purple coneflower."

**Contact herbicide:** This type of herbicide kills only the part of the plant that it touches, such as the leaves or the stems.

**Container:** Any pot or vessel that is used for planting; containers can be ceramic, clay, steel, or plastic—or a teacup, bucket, or barrel.

**Container garden:** This describes a garden that is created primarily by growing plants in containers instead of in the ground.

**Container grown:** This describes a plant that is grown, sold, and shipped while in a pot.

**Cool-season annual:** This is a flowering plant, such as snapdragon or pansy, that thrives during cooler months.

**Cool-season vegetable:** This is a vegetable, such as spinach, broccoli, and peas, that thrives during cooler months.

**Cover crop:** These plants are grown specifically to enrich the soil, prevent erosion, suppress weeds, and control pests and diseases.

**Cross-pollinate:** This describes the transfer of pollen from one plant to another plant.

**Dappled shade:** This is bright shade created by high tree branches or tree foliage, where patches of sunlight and shade intermingle.

**Day-neutral plant:** A plant that flowers when it reaches a certain size, regardless of the day length, is a day-neutral plant.

**Deadhead:** To remove dead flowers in order to encourage further bloom and prevent the plant from going to seed is to deadhead.

**Deciduous plant:** A plant that loses its leaves seasonally, typically in fall or early winter, is deciduous.

**Diatomaceous earth:** A natural control for snails, slugs, flea beetles, and other garden pests, diatomaceous earth consists of ground-up fossilized remains of sea creatures.

**Dormancy:** The period when plants stop growing in order to conserve energy, this happens naturally and seasonally, usually in winter.

**Drip line:** The ground area under the outer circumference of tree branches, this is where most of the tree's roots that absorb water and nutrients are found.

**Dwarf:** In the context of fruit gardening, a dwarf fruit tree is a tree that grows no taller than 10 feet tall and is usually a dwarf as a result of the rootstock of the tree.

**Evergreen:** A plant that keeps its leaves year-round, instead of dropping them seasonally is evergreen.

**Floating row covers:** Lightweight fabric that can be used to protect plants from pests. Usually white in color.

**Floricane:** A second-year cane on a blackberry or raspberry shrub; floricanes are fruit bearing.

**Flower stalk:** The stem that supports the flower and elevates it so that insects can reach the flower and pollinate it is the flower stalk.

**Four-tine claw:** Also called a cultivator, this hand tool typically has three to four curved tines and is used to break up soil clods or lumps before planting and to rake soil amendments into garden beds.

**Frost:** Ice crystals that form when the temperature falls below freezing (32°F) create frost.

**Full sun:** Areas of the garden that receive direct sunlight for six to eight hours a day or more, with no shade, are in full sun.

**Fungicide:** This describes a chemical compound used to control fungal diseases.

**Gallon container:** A standard nursery-sized container for plants, a gallon container is roughly equivalent to a gallon container of milk.

**Garden fork:** A garden implement with a long handle and short tines, use a garden fork for loosening and turning soil.

**Garden lime:** This soil amendment lowers soil acidity and raises the pH.

**Garden soil:** The existing soil in a garden bed; it is generally evaluated by its nutrient content and texture. Garden soil is also sold as a bagged item at garden centers and home-improvement stores.

**Germination:** This is the process by which a plant emerges from a seed or a spore.

**Grafted tree:** This is a tree composed of two parts: the top, or scion, which bears fruit, and the bottom, or rootstock.

**Graft union:** This is the place on a fruit tree trunk where the rootstock and the scion have been joined.

**Granular fertilizer:** This type of fertilizer comes in a dry, pellet-like form rather than a liquid or powder.

**Grass clippings:** The parts of grass that are removed when mowing, clippings are a valuable source of nitrogen for the lawn or the compost pile.

**Green materials:** An essential element in composting that includes grass clippings, kitchen scraps, and manure and provides valuable nitrogen in the pile, green materials are high in nitrogen.

**Hand pruners:** An important hand tool that consists of two sharp blades that perform a scissoring motion, these are used for light pruning, clipping, and cutting.

**Hardening off:** This is the process of slowly acclimating seedlings and young plants grown in an indoor environment to the outdoors.

**Hardiness zone map:** This map lists average annual minimum temperature ranges of a particular area. This information is helpful in determining appropriate plants for the garden. North America is divided into eleven separate hardiness zones.

**Hard rake:** This tool has a long handle and rigid tines at the bottom. It is great for moving a variety of garden debris, such as soil, mulch, leaves, and pebbles.

**Hedging:** This is the practice of trimming a line of plants to create a solid mass for privacy or garden definition.

**Heirloom:** A plant that was more commonly grown pre-World War II.

**Hoe:** A long-handled garden tool with a short, narrow, flat steel blade, it is used for breaking up hard soil and removing weeds.

**Hose breaker:** This device screws onto the end of a garden hose to disperse the flow of water from the hose.

**Host plant:** A plant grown to feed caterpillars that will eventually morph into butterflies is called a host plant.

**Hybrid:** Plants produced by crossing two genetically different plants, hybrids often have desirable characteristics such as disease resistance.

**Insecticide:** This substance is used for destroying or controlling insects that are harmful to plants. Insecticides are available in organic and synthetic forms.

**Irrigation:** A system of watering the landscape, irrigation can be an in-ground automatic system, soaker or drip hoses, or hand-held hoses with nozzles.

**Jute twine:** A natural-fiber twine, jute is used for gently staking plants or tying them to plant supports.

**Larva:** The immature stage of an insect that goes through complete metamorphosis; caterpillars are butterfly or moth larvae.

**Larvae:** This is the plural of larva.

**Leaf rake:** A long-handled rake with flexible tines on the head, a leaf rake is used for easily and efficiently raking leaves into piles.

**Liquid fertilizer:** Plant fertilizer in a liquid form, some types need to be mixed with water, and some types are ready to use from the bottle.

**Long-day plant:** Plants that flower when the days are longer than their critical photoperiod, long-day plants typically flower in early summer, when the days are still getting longer.

**Loppers:** One of the largest manual gardening tools, use loppers for pruning branches of 1 to 3 inches in diameter with a scissoring motion.

**Morning sun:** Areas of the garden that have an eastern exposure and receive direct sun in the morning hours are in morning sun.

**Mulch:** Any type of material that is spread over the soil surface around the base of plants to suppress weeds and retain soil moisture is mulch.

**Nematode:** Microscopic, wormlike organisms that live in the soil, some nematodes are beneficial, while others are harmful.

**New wood (new growth):** The new growth on plants, it is characterized by a greener, more tender form than older, woodier growth.

**Nozzle:** A device that attaches to the end of a hose and disperses water through a number of small holes; the resulting spray covers a wider area.

**Old wood:** Old wood is growth that is more than one year old. Some fruit plants produce on old wood. If you prune these plants in spring before they flower and fruit, you will cut off the wood that will produce fruit.

**Organic:** This term describes products derived from naturally occurring materials instead of materials synthesized in a lab.

**Part shade:** Areas of the garden that receive three to six hours of sun a day are in part shade. Plants requiring part shade will often require protection from the more intense afternoon sun, either from tree leaves or from a building.

**Part sun:** Areas of the garden that receive three to six hours of sun a day are in part sun. Although the term is often used interchangeably with "part shade," a "part sun" designation places greater emphasis on the minimal sun requirements.

**Perennial:** A plant that lives for more than two years is a perennial. Examples include trees, shrubs, and some flowering plants.

**pH:** A figure designating the acidity or the alkalinity of garden soil, pH is measured on a scale of 1 to 14, with 7.0 being neutral.

**Pinch:** This is a method to remove unwanted plant growth with your fingers, promoting bushier growth and increased blooming.

**Pitchfork:** A hand tool with a long handle and sharp metal prongs, a pitchfork is typically used for moving loose material such as mulch or hay.

**Plant label:** This label or sticker on a plant container provides a description of the plant and information on its care and growth habits.

**Pollination:** The transfer of pollen for fertilization from the male pollen-bearing structure (stamen) to the female structure (pistil), usually by wind, bees, butterflies, moths, or hummingbirds; this process is required for fruit production.

**Potting soil:** A mixture used to grow flowers, herbs, and vegetables in containers, potting soil provides proper drainage and extra nutrients for healthy growth.

**Powdery mildew:** A fungal disease characterized by white powdery spots on plant leaves and stems, this disease is worse during times of drought or when plants have poor air circulation.

**Power edger:** This electric or gasoline-powered edger removes grass along flower beds and walkways for a neat appearance.

**Pre-emergent herbicide:** This weedkiller works by preventing weed seeds from sprouting.

**Primocane:** A first-year cane on a blackberry shrub, a primocane doesn't produce fruit.

**Pruning:** This is a garden task in which a variety of hand tools are used to remove dead or overgrown branches to increase plant fullness and health.

**Pruning saw:** This hand tool for pruning smaller branches and limbs features a long, serrated blade with an elongated handle.

**Rhizome:** An underground horizontal stem that grows side shoots, a rhizome is similar to a bulb.

**Rootball:** The network of roots and soil clinging to a plant when it is lifted out of the ground is the rootball.

**Rootstock:** The bottom part of a grafted fruit tree, rootstocks are often used to create dwarf fruit trees, impart pest or disease resistance, or make a plant more cold hardy.

**Runner:** A stem sprouting from the center of a strawberry plant, a runner produces fruit in its second year.

**Scaffold branch:** This horizontal branch emerges almost perpendicular to the trunk.

**Scientific name:** This two-word identification system consists of the genus and species of a plant, such as *Ilex opaca*.

**Scion:** The top, fruit-bearing part of a grafted fruit tree is the scion.

**Scissors:** A two-bladed hand tool great for cutting cloth, paper, twine, and other lightweight materials, scissors are a basic garden tool.

**Seed packet:** The package in which vegetable and flower seeds are sold, it typically includes growing instructions, a planting chart, and harvesting information.

**Seed-starting mix:** Typically a soilless blend of perlite, vermiculite, peat moss, and other ingredients, seed-starting mix is specifically formulated for growing plants from seed.

**Self-fertile:** A plant that does not require cross-pollination from another plant in order to produce fruit is self-fertile.

**Semidwarf:** A fruit tree grafted onto a rootstock that restricts growth of the tree to one-half to two-thirds of its natural size is semidwarf.

**Shade:** Garden shade is the absence of any direct sunlight in a given area, usually due to tree foliage or building shadows.

**Short-day plant:** Flowering when the length of day is shorter than its critical photoperiod, short-day plants typically bloom during fall, winter, or early spring.

**Shovel:** A handled tool with a broad, flat blade and slightly upturned sides, used for moving soil and other garden materials, a shovel is a basic garden tool.

**Shredded hardwood mulch:** A mulch consisting of shredded wood that interlocks, resisting washout and suppressing weeds, hardwood mulch can change soil pH.

**Shrub:** This woody plant is distinguished from a tree by its multiple trunks and branches and its shorter height of less than 15 feet tall.

**Shrub rake:** This long-handled rake with a narrow head fits easily into tight spaces between plants.

**Sidedress:** To sprinkle slow-release fertilizer along the side of a plant row or plant stem is to sidedress.

**Slow-release fertilizer:** This form of fertilizer releases nutrients at a slower rate throughout the season, requiring less-frequent applications.

**Snips:** This hand tool, used for snipping small plants and flowers, is perfect for harvesting fruits, vegetables, and flowers.

**Soaker hose:** This is an efficient watering system in which a porous hose, usually made from recycled rubber, allows water to seep out around plant roots.

**Soil knife:** This garden knife with a sharp, serrated edge, is used for cutting twine, plant roots, turf, and other garden materials.

**Soil test:** An analysis of a soil sample, this determines the level of nutrients (to identify deficiencies) and detects pH.

**Spade:** This short-handled tool with a sharp, rectangular metal blade is used for cutting and digging soil or turf.

**Spur:** This is a small, compressed, fruit-bearing branch on a fruit tree.

**Standard:** Describing a fruit tree grown on its own seedling rootstock or a nondwarfing rootstock, this is the largest of the three sizes of fruit trees.

**Sucker:** The odd growth from the base of a tree or a woody plant, often caused by stress, this also refers to sprouts from below the graft of a rose or fruit tree. Suckers divert energy away from the desirable tree growth and should be removed.

**Systemic herbicide:** This type of weedkiller is absorbed by the plant's roots and taken into the roots to destroy all parts of the plant.

**Taproot:** This is an enlarged, tapered plant root that grows vertically downward.

**Thinning:** This is the practice of removing excess vegetables (root crops) to leave more room for the remaining vegetables to grow; also refers to the practice of removing fruits when still small from fruit trees so that the remaining fruits can grow larger.

**Topdress:** To spread fertilizer on top of the soil (usually around fruit trees or vegetables) is to topdress.

**Transplants:** Plants that are grown in one location and then moved to and replanted in another, seeds started indoors and nursery plants are two examples.

**Tree:** This woody perennial plant typically consists of a single trunk with multiple lateral branches.

**Tree canopy:** This is the upper layer of growth, consisting of the tree's branches and leaves.

**Tropical plant:** This is a plant that is native to a tropical region of the world, and thus acclimated to a warm, humid climate and not hardy to frost.

**Trowel:** This shovel-like hand tool is used for digging or moving small amounts of soil.

**Warm-season vegetable:** This is a vegetable that thrives during the warmer months. Examples are tomatoes, okra, and peppers. These vegetables do not tolerate frost.

**Watering wand:** This hose attachment features a longer handle for watering plants beyond reach.

**Water sprout:** This vertical shoot emerges from a scaffold branch. It is usually nonfruiting and undesirable.

**Wheat straw:** These dry stalks of wheat, which are used for mulch, retain soil moisture and suppress weeds.

**Wood chips:** Small pieces of wood made by cutting or chipping, wood chips are used as mulch in the garden.

# INDEX

# PHOTO CREDITS

Tom Eltzroth: pp. 88, 99, 224

Katie Elzer-Peters: pp. 9, 10, 12, 20, 22, 23 (top), 25, 26, 28, 29 (both), 30 (all), 32, 34 (all), 35 (all), 36 (all), 37 (all), 38 (all), 41, 42, 43, 44 (both), 45, 46, 50, 52 (all), 53 (all), 54 (all), 55 (all), 56, 57, 58 (both), 59, 60, 61 (both), 62, 66, 70, 81 (top three), 84 (all), 91, 131, 140, 145, 146, 148, 150, 155, 160, 172, 176, 180, 181, 183, 184, 185, 186, 188, 189, 191, 193, 199, 202, 204, 205, 208, 214, 215, 217, 219, 220, 226, 232, 236, 237,

iStock: 23 (bottom), 71, 74, 76, 81 (bottom), 92 (both), 97, 101, 102, 103, 114, 119, 124, 128, 136, 156, 164, 166, 168, 174, 177, 203, 210, 223, 229, 234, 235,

Jupiter Images: pp. 98, 201

Leu Gardens, City of Orlando: pp. 73, 120

Shutterstock: pp. 51, 79, 94, 96, 105, 108, 109, 117, 118, 138, 152, 159, 162, 171, 194, 196, 207, 213, 225, 227, 231,

Photo courtesy of Stark Bro's., www.starkbros.com: pp. 86, 87

Lynn Steiner: pp. 8, 178, 218, 222, 228

Superstock: pp. 77

Thinkstock: pp.126

# MEET KATIE ELZER-PETERS

Gardening is a hobby-turned-career for Katie Elzer-Peters, one her parents and grandparents nurtured in her since she could walk. After receiving a bachelor's of science in public horticulture from Purdue University, Katie completed the Longwood Graduate Program at Longwood Gardens and the University of Delaware, receiving a master's of science in public garden management.

Katie has served as a horticulturist, head of gardens, educational programs director, development officer, and manager of botanical gardens around the United States, including the Washington Park Arboretum in Seattle, Washington; the Indianapolis Zoo in Indianapolis, Indiana; the Marie Selby Botanical Garden in Sarasota, Florida; the Smithsonian Institution in Washington, DC; Longwood Gardens in Kennett Square, Pennsylvania; Winterthur Museum, Garden, and Library in Greenville, Delaware; the King's Garden at Fort Ticonderoga in Ticonderoga, New York; and Airlie Gardens in Wilmington, North Carolina.

Whether at a botanical garden, or for a garden center, garden club, or school group, Katie has shared her love of gardening by teaching classes and workshops and writing brochures, articles, gardening website information, and columns. While serving as curator of landscape at Fort Ticonderoga, Katie planned and led garden bus tours along the east coast of the United States and Canada.

Today, Katie lives and gardens with her husband and their dog in the coastal city of Wilmington, North Carolina (zone 8a). She loves the year-round weather for gardening but is in constant battle with the sandy soil. Katie manages GreatGardenSpeakers.com, an online speaker directory of garden, design, ecology, and horticultural speakers. She also owns the Garden of Words, LLC, a marketing and PR firm specializing in garden-industry clients.

Katie is the author of *Beginner's Illustrated Guide to Gardening: Techniques to Help You Get Started*, also published by Cool Springs Press.